WINGS *of* FAITH

Books by Dawn Volz:

Saved! The Salvos' guide to the good life

Will & Kate: The story of William & Catherine Booth

Books by Harry Read:

Words of Life 1992-2002

No Heart More Tender

Heart Talk

Language of the Soul

WINGS of FAITH

THE REMARKABLE LIFE OF **HARRY READ**

DAWN VOLZ

ISBN 978-0-646-85901-9

First published 2022

Design and layout:
Richard Lewis

Sincere and grateful thanks to John and Anne Read,
Margaret Ord, Ken Lawson and Doug Kollmorgen
for their invaluable help in reading and commenting
on the manuscript of *Wings of Faith*.

~

Thanks also to David Goodwin for information
and advice about online publishing.

They that wait upon the Lord … shall mount up with wings as eagles; they shall run and not be weary, and they shall walk and not faint.

~ ISAIAH 40:31

FOREWORD

If I referred to a 'King's Messenger', many people might first think of a spokesperson for a monarch or perhaps an angelic being representing God in significant moments. But in this Foreword to *Wings of Faith*, I refer to Commissioner Harry Read as a King's Messenger, as it identifies him with those who shared a sessional name as they trained to be Salvation Army officers in 1947–48.

Key to understanding Harry's dramatic life story is a knowledge of how it is intertwined with his lifetime of ministry in the Army. In my view, whilst *Wings of Faith* provides an excellent record of a King's Messenger, it could never fully capture the full impact of Harry's life, because much of his influence is recorded only in the heavenly record.

> *"For I know the plans I have for you," declares the Lord,*
> *"...plans to give you hope and a future" (Jeremiah 29:11).*

God had captured Harry's heart long before he responded to the call to train as a Salvation Army officer, and it was this dramatic, divine reality that set the course for a lifetime of outstanding service.

A further key milestone for Harry occurred when he met and fell in love with a south Yorkshire girl, Winifred Humphries. Together they moved about the world, giving decades of influential leadership and ministry. A personal memory was meeting them while they served in Canada, and we experienced the impact of their ministry. Having listened to them speak, we were further enamoured by the pleasant, engaging, gentle exchange that was pastoral, encouraging and challenging. They walked, spoke and ministered together as they drew upon each other's strengths, making themselves fully available to the God they served.

This book spans four decades of ministry given by Commissioners Harry and Win Read. If you look closely, you will see each appointment increasing in responsibility. Each time they were selected for greater service, Harry and Win reflected consistent and growing capacity and, consequently, value to The Salvation Army. Their reputations were so unswerving that confidence in them brought positions of influence both at home and abroad.

I reconnected with Commissioner Harry in his retirement journey, although there was little evidence of him slowing down or being less influential! He captured our hearts on many occasions – one example being his 75th anniversary D-Day parachute jump in 2019. I recall his interview following the jump, admiring his creative use of words and the fact that he always gave honour and glory to God.

It was this life of serving his heavenly Father that prompted the award of The Salvation Army's highest honour, the Order of the Founder, also in 2019. As General, it was a personal delight to again stand on a platform with Harry and acknowledge this humble servant.

You will be inspired by *Wings of Faith*. It beautifully captures the story of this man and his dedication to God. I hope we will each aspire to live such a life.

While writing these few words, news has come of Commissioner Harry Read's promotion to Glory. Immediately I whispered the words: "Well done, good and faithful servant." On behalf of a grateful Salvation Army, I thank God for the life of Harry Read, truly a King's Messenger, who has now risen on the wings of faith into the arms of God.

I commend this book to you and thank Dawn for recording this man and his story.

~ BRIAN PEDDLE
General of The Salvation Army

PREFACE

I first met Commissioner Harry Read in February 2013 when reading Major Stephen Court's online *Journal of Aggressive Christianity* in which Harry participated in an in-depth interview about his life. Reading of his wartime service as a 20-year-old wireless operator who parachuted into France on D-Day in 1944, I was captivated and thought, "This Commissioner has a story to tell!"

Then I read about his many years at The Salvation Army's International Training College, and his overseas service in Canada and Australia, followed by his appointment as British Commissioner. I was intrigued and looked to see if his name came up on Facebook. There it was, including the poems for which he has become renowned and which have blessed so many, including me.

I also noted the many Facebook comments urging Harry to publish a book of his poems. As I was the assistant literary secretary of The Salvation Army's Australia Southern Territory, a light bulb clicked on in my head. I presented my proposal for the territory to publish an anthology of Harry's poems and the suggestion was readily taken up by the Literary Council, under the leadership of Captain Mal Davies.

I found an email address but, before presenting the proposal, wanted to confirm that the recipient was indeed Commissioner Harry Read. Back came the prompt answer, with typical wit: "I am the guilty party!" Within months a book of Harry's poems, titled *Heart Talk: The Give and Take of Communion with God* was produced by Salvo Publishing, and launched at a Sunday morning meeting at Winton Bournemouth, Harry's home corps, when I was delighted to be present.

From that time on Harry and I became online penpals, with weekly missives being exchanged via email. Never one to blow his own trumpet, it took years of wheedling, encouragement and coaxing to convince him that his is a story that needs to be told.

Recently retired, I thought to myself, "What better way to spend early retirement than chronicling the life story of Commissioner Harry Read!"

As we live on opposite sides of the world, there were many hours of emails, phone calls and FaceTimes between Melbourne and Bournemouth in a lively collaboration. Harry's prodigious memory, wit and wisdom made these happy and enjoyable times.

My hope is that you will be encouraged, blessed and inspired as you read about the remarkable life and vibrant faith of Commissioner Harry Read.

~ DAWN VOLZ

CONTENTS

1

A GODLY HERITAGE

Give me the child until he is seven and I will show you the man.

~ ARISTOTLE

The year 1924 was seemingly a fortuitous one for Britain. With memories of the misery and deprivation of World War I receding into the past, the Roaring Twenties were in full swing and there was an air of hedonism among the upper classes.

Britain was the Mother Country of a worldwide empire which covered a fifth of the land in the world. The spectacular 1924-25 British Empire Exhibition at London's Wembley Park, opened by King George V, was attracting huge crowds, with 56 of 58 nations that comprised the empire participating, each featuring a distinctive pavilion reflecting local culture and architecture. This huge exhibition attracted 18 million visitors in 1924, although when the exhibition closed in 1925 it had made a loss of £1.5 million.

Seemingly oblivious to – or in spite of – the clouds on the economic horizon and the spectre of mass unemployment, particularly in the north of England, Britain celebrated.

This was the world that welcomed the infant Harry Read, born in Teesville, situated east of Middlesbrough in North Yorkshire, on 17 May 1924, the third child of Robert and Florence Read. Teesville was a small, rather unimaginatively named town located south of the River Tees. The surrounding valley had become industrialised and families from all over the United Kingdom had poured in to find employment.

Both Harry's parents were dedicated soldiers of The Salvation Army (formerly known as the Christian Mission), a movement that had galvanised the country since 1865. This vibrant, revolutionary expression of Christianity, begun under the dynamic leadership of the founders, William and Catherine Booth, was to become central to his life during the coming years.

Harry's paternal grandfather, Robert Read, born in 1838, had been an agricultural labourer – as was his family before him – in Norfolk before moving to Hartlepool, a coastal town just north of the Tees, in search of employment in the booming town. Robert, then in his late 30s, was converted under the ministry of James 'Fiddler' Dowdell, a violin-playing preacher who attracted attention by wearing a plume-feathered helmet. Larger-than-life and a powerful speaker, Dowdell was sent by William Booth, under the auspices of the Christian Mission, to the north of England with the order to win converts and open mission stations.

When the Christian Mission became The Salvation Army in 1878, Robert Read served as the corps sergeant major of the local corps. Later moving from Hartlepool to South Bank, a newly-built town on the south side of the river, in order to find employment at the large steelworks there, he became the sergeant major of the South Bank Corps, ultimately fulfilling the role of honorary sergeant major, with a total of 38 years' service.

Robert Read had a large family of eight children but his wife Sarah died when he was in his early fifties, and he married again, to Lucy Price, a widow with five children, in 1891. After adding a daughter to the family in 1892, at the age of 57 Robert welcomed Harry's father, Robert Jnr. Because Lucy could neither read nor write, she registered the birth of her newborns by signing the paperwork with an 'X', which the registrar countersigned to give it validation. Lucy died of tuberculosis when Robert was eight years old.

Once he became converted, Robert Snr, who had never attended school, learned to read as a result of his frequent use of the Bible and singing from the Salvation Army song book. He died at the age of 85 in 1924 – the year of Harry's birth – from injuries sustained after being run over by a motorcyclist.

Following in his father's footsteps, in the 1930s Harry's father, Robert Jnr, was appointed as the corps sergeant major at South

Bank. Robert had met Florence McAdam, Harry's mother, at the corps and they were married on 24 May 1919. Short of stature, strict, stern and hardworking, Robert had a strong sense of duty, a mindset he instilled in his children by his firm example.

Florence had become a Salvationist as a teenager, and following her conversion other members of the McAdam family, including her parents, became soldiers. She and Robert welcomed three children in four years – Wilfred in September 1921, Lucy 20 months later in May 1923, and Harry in May 1924. Florence was gracious, kind and loving, a dedicated mother who always put her children first.

Harry's maternal grandfather, Francis McAdam, came from Musselburgh in Scotland, on the coast of the Firth of Forth. He was a rigger on merchant ships that sailed around the coast of England. When Francis met Ellen Bedingfield in Norfolk, they fell in love, married, and settled down to have a family. With furnaces being built for the iron ore business, Francis got a job as a rigger at a processing plant, assembling equipment and erecting scaffolding, and eventually becoming a foreman. The McAdam family, with five children, lived at Eston Grange, not far from Teesville.

At the time of Harry's birth his parents were completely dependent on unemployment benefits. Robert, then unmarried, had served for almost four years with the 12th and 5th Battalions of the Yorkshire Regiment – also known as the Green Howards – in World War I, and Florence had worked in a munitions factory. Robert was twice wounded and hospitalised and, following the Armistice, returned to a country which, in the politicians' turn of phrase, would be "a land fit for heroes to live in". That promise rang hollow for those who, like Robert Read, returned to endure unemployment and poverty.

The Read family spent the first few years of Harry's life living on a council estate in a severely depressed area, with Robert and Florence struggling to make a comfortable life for themselves and their children. The small, sparse, semi-detached house in which they lived was of necessity shared with another family, Mr and Mrs King and their son Gordon, who was the same age as Harry.

One of Harry's earliest recollections is of being taken for a walk by his mother and the other lady of the house, who he called Mummy King, to the farmer's meadow across the road from their house. When they were chased by an enraged gander, honking loudly and flapping his huge wings, the ladies were startled and afraid but Harry distinctly remembers being unfazed – curious rather than frightened. That inherent fearlessness was a sign of things to come.

Robert continually tried to get work and Florence helped to make ends meet by stitching clothes for the children on a second-hand sewing machine which she and Robert had scrimped and scraped to purchase. Meals were often meagre, but Harry especially enjoyed helpings of Yorkshire pudding soaked in gravy, the accompaniment for perhaps a meal of vegetable soup. Grace was always said before meals, no matter the scarcity of food.

"We were very poor, we were all very poor," Harry says. "As children we hardly noticed it, but our parents must have been cruelly hard-pressed. Unemployment reached 70 per cent in some areas at the start of the 1930s and the Great Depression, and families depended on the dole, paid by the local government."

Despite the family's straitened circumstances, as a blond-haired, blue-eyed, mischievous young lad, Harry's childhood was carefree. He has treasured memories of kicking up his heels enjoying happy-go-lucky days with his elder brother Wilf, who he adored – and who he describes as a superb role model – and his sister Lucy. He especially enjoyed playing football and cricket with Wilf, who was an excellent sportsman.

From his earliest childhood Harry grew up in The Salvation Army, attending the meetings with his sergeant major father, mother and siblings – never absent, never late – each Sunday. And the Sabbath was anything but a day of rest. There were morning, afternoon and evening open air meetings for the parents, with concurrent activities for the children, in addition to an 11 am holiness meeting, 2 pm praise meeting and 7 pm salvation meeting.

Harry's father took his corps sergeant major's responsibilities seriously. Under his guidance, the open air meeting, during which bystanders would be invited to join the Salvationists at their indoor service, started exactly on time, and latecomers were frowned upon.

When Harry was four years old the family moved to a council house in Grangetown. They continued to attend South Bank Corps, walking the mile and a half to the hall, so of necessity on Sundays they took their meals with them. Eventually they transferred to the local Grangetown Corps, just two streets away from their home. Florence's widowed mother Ellen, who lived in a bungalow across the road from them, also attended the corps.

Harry remembers that his grandmother had two massive pictures hanging in the small hallway of her retirement cottage. As the front door opened, William Booth looked down imperiously from the right and Catherine gazed more compassionately from the left, both in full regimentals. Harry always behaved himself at Grandma's.

"I'm the product of good, loving, dedicated Salvationist parents and grandparents to whom I'm enormously indebted," he says.

Inquisitive and bright, when it was time to start school at age five Harry was more than ready to begin his education. By the 1920s State primary education was free and children were required to attend from 9 am to 4.30 pm. Harry attended the Grangetown Board School run by the local authority, situated in an old Victorian building with rather primitive conditions. He took to his chalk and slate like a duck to water and enjoyed school to the full.

Being a natural left-hander, however, didn't come without its problems. Compelled to write with his right hand at school, under the threat of a sharp rap on the knuckles for surreptitiously changing hands, he nevertheless switched when he thought he was unobserved. His headmaster, an exceptionally tall, uncompromising disciplinarian, was always on the lookout for miscreants.

In the classroom one day, Harry became conscious of a tall presence standing close to him and the headmaster's voice, from on high, saying, "I see you're writing with your left hand, Read." "Yes, Sir," Harry confessed, adding by way of justification, "I can't write with my right hand, Sir." With superb timing, the headmaster waited for a moment or two before archly replying, "You can't write with your left hand either!" Although crestfallen, Harry couldn't repress a wry smile as the headmaster continued on his way.

A confident and independent boy, Harry enjoyed stretching the boundaries at school, and he was no stranger to the cane. Never lost for words, he had a quick wit and delighted in "making the lads laugh" during class, much to the chagrin of the teachers. So the cane it was, but he was unflinching, enduring the pain while stoically keeping a smile on his face.

At the age of seven and a half, on a Decision Sunday at the corps, Harry gave his heart to Jesus and became a junior soldier of The Salvation Army, promising to be faithful and live as a loving and obedient child of Jesus for the rest of his life.

Soon afterwards, Harry was co-opted into the young people's band at the corps. His father was a good instrumentalist and wanted Harry to play trombone. He supervised Harry's practice, digging him in the ribs as he said, "You played a wrong note." Unperturbed, Harry would answer, "I know I did." "Well, why did you play it then?" All Harry could do was look at his dad with a bemused smile. By his own admission, he was never a musician – words were his passion.

Not surprisingly, his favourite subject at school was literature. He remembers one teacher, Miss Netta Jones, who taught classic poems that captured his imagination. The words became embedded in his mind, as Miss Jones decreed that her pupils memorise a verse of the poem they were discussing and recite it back to her in five minutes' time, a task in which Harry excelled. He became an avid reader, exhausting the resources of the school library, and opting to visit the public library, a mile away, to browse through their selection of books.

School was not the only preoccupation of this industrious boy, and the year Harry turned eight was a singular one. He was keen to join the local Baden-Powell Wolf Cub pack but it cost three-pence per week. He asked permission from his father, who said, "Harry, we don't have threepence a week. Perhaps you could try to get a job as a paper boy." Just 300 or 400 yards from the Read house was a tiny row of shops, including a newsagent/post office. Harry approached Mr Young, the owner, and despite his young age was promptly hired.

The Read household had only one clock, an alarm that sat on the mantelpiece. At night Harry's father would take the clock upstairs with him in order to wake to the alarm and rouse young Harry in time for him to be at the railway station – "a country mile distant", Harry says – at 6 am to collect the newspapers that he would deliver before going to school. Harry used to hand the papers to the newsagent who, while Harry nipped home for some breakfast, addressed them for distribution. Back on his bike, Harry would return to set out on the task of delivering them to the news-starved locals.

At such a young age this six-days-a-week job was a huge responsibility but not once did Harry shirk his duties. Early mornings saw him pedalling to the station to collect the large bundle of newspapers, putting them in a strong hessian bag, placing the straps around his neck and balancing the bag on the handlebars. Rain, hail, shine – or even snow and ice – did not deter Harry from his deliveries and he was the local paperboy for the next five years. This driving energy and zest for self-discipline and hard work was to become the hallmark of Harry's life.

Now able to pay his own way, Harry joined the local Wolf Cub pack, responding with the other boys to the command "Dyb dyb dyb" (do your best) by shouting "We'll dob dob dob" (do our best), and proudly wearing the distinctive uniform, including cap and neckerchief. Cubs also promised to "do their duty to God and the King ... and do a good turn to somebody every day".

Three years later Harry graduated to the Boy Scouts and, as well as learning teamwork, leadership, camping skills, cooking, first aid, etc., was required to follow the Scout promises:

A Scout's honour is to be trusted. ✓
A Scout is loyal to the King and to his officers, and to his country, and to his employers. ✓

A Scout's duty is to be useful and to help others. ✓
A Scout is a friend to all and a brother to every other Scout, no matter to what social class the other belongs. ✓
A Scout is courteous. ✓
A Scout is a friend to animals. ✓
A Scout obeys orders of his patrol leader or Scoutmaster without question. ✓
A Scout smiles and whistles under all difficulties. ✓
A Scout is thrifty. ✓
A Scout is clean in thought, word and deed. ✓

Harry diligently ticked all the boxes, embracing disciplines that were to stand him in good stead for the rest of his life. Scouting was as important to his formation as his Salvation Army background and he was allowed to attend camps and other activities even though it meant missing out on Salvation Army duties, as a Sunday service was held by the Scouts. As part of his Scout training, he also learned how to communicate using semaphore and Morse code. Little did he know that finessing these skills was to become the catalyst for a future calling to service for his country.

In 1935, at age 11, Harry attended the brand-new Sir William Worsley Secondary Modern School, proud to be one of its first pupils. His father Robert, after years of intermittent casual labour, became the caretaker at the school, attending to the cleaning and maintenance of the buildings, and from this time the family never looked back. It was fortunate that Harry's father was employed, as at this time Florence had given birth to another son, who they named John.

Harry enjoyed good health during his childhood, and was fortunate not to contract measles, mumps or whooping cough, but he frequently suffered from tonsillitis, with a sore throat and difficulty in swallowing. At around age 12, the discomfort was so severe that Harry's mother took him to the local doctor. After hearing the doctor's declaration, "We'll have to think about taking your tonsils out", Harry never had tonsillitis again!

He loved all kinds of sport and played football, cricket and rounders. His brother Wilf was an excellent all-round sportsman and a brilliant footballer, chosen at 14 to play for Yorkshire. Wilf's dreams were dashed when his father decreed that he was to become an apprentice blacksmith, and Harry began to wonder what his own working future would hold. However, with his early-morning paper round, school, Scouts and Salvation Army activities, his days were full, and there was little time to ponder such things.

As he approached adolescence, Harry grew and blossomed. His young life had not been without its challenges, but never in his wildest dreams could he have foreseen what his late teenage years were to bring.

2

EARNING HIS WINGS

The more grounded you are the higher you fly.

~ J.R. RIM

A fine Yorkshire lad, Harry began his adolescence seemingly without a care in the world, with school, Scouts and The Salvation Army continuing to be his main preoccupations. The tumultuous events of the next decade, however, were to define his manhood and leave an indelible stamp on his young life.

Full of energy, he retained his job of delivering the morning newspapers to the townsfolk before arriving, smartly uniformed and on time, at secondary school. Always keen to be involved, he played every available sport at school and revelled in the literature classes, with his early love of reading unabated. "Captain James Cook was born not far from my birthplace. What a navigator! What courage! In my reading and imagination, I've travelled every mile with him," Harry says.

He was also captivated by the story of Captain Robert Falcon Scott, a Royal Navy officer and explorer who from 1910-1913 led the ill-fated *Terra Nova* expedition to the South Pole. Harry says Scott's return journey, though ending in his death and those of his colleagues, was "an epic failure and full of courage". As Harry matured, books continued to absorb him and, as well as Bible study, his Christian faith in his late teenage years was hugely influenced by author C.S. Lewis, "a living legend and a giant of the faith, whose books gave my faith a great deal of substance".

Harry enjoyed his Scouting activities to the full – he was a patrol leader and had many strong friendships with his fellow Scouts. He especially enjoyed camping, signalling and canoeing, and over the years kept his mother busy sewing 18 achievement badges on his uniform. He became a King's Scout and also earned the Bushman's Thong, another high award. Harry continued to attend The Salvation Army with his parents and family, but whenever he could he joined many of his Scouting friends, either at weekend camps in the summer, or in Sunday meetings at the Methodist Church.

By the time he was 12, the Read family had acquired a mantel radio, and a whole new world of news, information and entertainment opened up for them. Five days before Harry's 13th birthday, on 12 May 1937, the family listened to the BBC broadcast of the coronation of King George VI. Harry was intrigued by the history and the personalities involved, and full of admiration for George VI, who stepped into the breach after the abdication of his older brother Edward VIII.

Harry also remembers his visits to the local cinema, wide-eyed as he watched the 'talkies' that had replaced the silent films of the 1920s. For Salvationists, cinema-going was – if not forbidden – very much frowned upon and Harry's parents were disapproving. However, after a few forays to the movies, when his parents realised he had not suddenly become a child of the devil, permission was more frequently, if not too happily, given.

At this time, changes were happening in the Read household. Harry's brother Wilf, now 17, asked his father's permission to leave his blacksmith's job and join the British Army. Robert Read was adamant: "You'll never get my signature!" was his blunt retort. He had seldom spoken about his wartime experiences, despite having signed up as a volunteer and serving with the Green Howards in World War I, including massive battles in the Somme and Ypres.

Robert had been twice wounded in battle, and after recovering in hospital was sent back for more of the same. His feelings ran deep – the family later discovered from military records that he had declined to accept the Victory Medal, presumably because of the devastating impact of war on his life.

Wilf, however, was determined and eventually persuaded his father to allow him to sign up for military service. He joined East

Yorkshire Regiment Headquarters, quickly progressing from lance corporal and corporal to sergeant. When it became obvious that war was looming and that officer personnel needed to be augmented by non-public school graduates, Wilf was chosen for the first officer cadet training unit. As a newly-commissioned officer in the Royal Artillery he served in desert battles in the Middle East, and then in Sicily, before eventually returning to the UK.

As for Lucy, at age 14 she became one of the 25 per cent of employed women in Britain who went into domestic service. She worked at a fine doctor's home where she was treated as one of the family and remained in their service until being conscripted at 18 into the Women's Auxiliary Air Force (WAAF).

In the meantime, Harry felt the pull of the Methodist Church and his many friends there. After much persuasion by him, and with serious reservations, his parents reluctantly allowed him to leave The Salvation Army and formally join the Methodist Church.

Four months after Harry celebrated his 15th birthday, at 11.15 am on 3 September 1939, came the Declaration of War by Prime Minister Neville Chamberlain, following the German invasion of Poland two days earlier. Harry and his parents were gathered around the radio at the time, and the announcement came as no surprise to a nation that had been on tenterhooks for weeks, with the spectre of war increasingly imminent.

When the local schools closed temporarily because of the war, Harry left at age 15, wanting to do something to contribute to the war effort. The interviewer at the Labour Exchange told Harry he had the very job for him, and he started his working life at Smith's Dock, a local shipbuilding company.

Too young to become an apprentice, he was employed as a 'marker boy', assisting tradesmen involved in shaping, bending and punching rivet holes in large sheets of steel. The hours were 7.30 am to 5 pm, with a half-hour lunch break, Monday to Friday, and a half day on Saturday, for which Harry was paid the princely sum of nine shillings and seven pence. It was not to his liking – he hated the factory environment and the constant, jarring noise – but in spite of his discomfort he was conscientious and hardworking.

Having achieved all he could in the Boy Scouts, and with an eye to future military service, Harry joined the local squadron of the Air Defence Cadet Corps (later to become the Air Training Corps), set up to attract those who had an interest in aviation. Ever since he was a young boy making home-made kites with Wilf and being entranced by aircraft displays in his town, flying held a fascination for him. The cadets were given as much service and aviation background as possible, as well as instruction in drills and discipline.

Also at this time, Harry had a growing conviction that he should assist in the Methodist local ministry. Since one of his older friends was a Methodist local preacher, Harry made a similar application and, in 1940, aged 16, became a 'local preacher on note'. This meant that an older local preacher would mentor him and Harry would accompany him to his Sunday preaching engagements, read the Bible passages and lead a hymn or two. He was greatly influenced by his mentor, Mr Croudace, a wise, godly man who he liked and respected.

After manning up at the shipbuilders for six months, Harry resigned when it was mooted that an Essential Work Order, which tied workers to jobs considered essential for the war effort, was to become law.

Relishing the opportunity for a change of employment, he got a job as a costing clerk at the local offices of a meat importer, the Wholesale Meat Supply Association, a company that was losing many employees because of conscription. The position was better paid and much more to Harry's liking. After a few months, the chairman offered him a promotion at their Malton offices, 41 miles from Grangetown, with excellent pay and accommodation provided.

With his parents' blessing, Harry made the move to Malton and was accommodated in a large house, the occupants including an infantry regimental sergeant major, Albert Stephenson, his wife and small daughter. Whenever duties permitted, Albert visited his wife and child and gave Harry good advice concerning his future military service. Their friendship endured over the coming years.

Harry eventually left the Air Defence Cadet Corps and joined the Home Guard, set up for men below or above the age of conscription and those unfit for front-line military service. The Home Guard increasingly provided useful training for younger men before their call-up to the Army.

Moving to Malton did not mean that Harry abandoned his calling to preach in the Methodist Church. From its earliest days Methodism had ordained ministers whose ministry was ably augmented by local preachers, so Harry was co-opted to cycle anywhere up to 20 miles away to singlehandedly lead the Sunday service and deliver the sermon at small Methodist churches, largely to the delight of the friendly local congregation.

With Harry's 18th birthday approaching, his thoughts turned once again to serving his country, as conscription was compulsory for those aged between 18 and 41. He was keen to volunteer earlier but his father refused to give his consent, as Wilf was a commissioned officer in the Royal Artillery and Lucy was in the WAAF and Robert reckoned that was enough.

Harry's RSM friend Albert, knowing that he was adept at Morse code, advised him to volunteer for the Royal Corps of Signals. So when Harry visited his family to celebrate his upcoming 18th birthday he said to his father, "Dad, whether you like it or not I'm going to be conscripted. If you give me permission to join up voluntarily before then I can go as a wireless operator and they will honour that." His father was placated and signed the necessary paperwork.

Four months later, in September 1942, Harry joined the Royal Signals, with training being held in Prestatyn, North Wales. As a rookie, along with the other raw recruits, he was given a regulation short-back-and-sides haircut and issued with a uniform before undertaking six weeks of basic training, plus aptitude and intelligence tests.

Harry must have impressed, as for a time he held the title of unpaid acting local lance corporal, prior to being nominated for officer cadet training. At a subsequent interview he was told that there was a need for infantry officers, but his abiding ambition was to work as a wireless operator. "Sir," he told the interviewing officer,

"I would rather stay with the Signals than go to the officer cadet training unit to be an officer elsewhere."

Then followed six months of intensive wireless operator training, during which trainees were regularly tested for speed and accuracy in sending and receiving Morse code messages. Calling on his Scout training in Morse code's dots and dashes, Harry excelled as a wireless operator, achieving impressive speeds.

Early in 1943, it was announced by a posting on the noticeboard that a new Airborne Division was being formed and they were seeking wireless operators. With his background in the Air Defence Cadet Corps, Harry volunteered immediately, the only one of the wireless operators to put his name down.

As part of the para assessment procedure, Major Donald of the Royal Corps of Signals interviewed Harry, endeavouring to dispel any romantic notions of parachuting. His introductory spiel fell on deaf ears where Harry was concerned. "You know it's far more dangerous crossing a road than it is jumping out of an aeroplane and dangling at the end of a parachute," the major intoned. "I am volunteering, Sir," Harry replied, "I don't need to be persuaded."

On completion of his wireless training and passing out parade in May of that year, Signalman Harry Read was assigned to the 6th Airborne Division, which had been formed on 7 May. He joined the division on 25 May, having just turned 19, and was posted to Bulford Camp on Salisbury Plain, for some time the youngest man in the unit.

On arrival, Harry was disappointed to find that he had been incorrectly recorded as a volunteer for the Air Landing (gliderborne) Brigade, an error he immediately reported. In the meantime, he undertook two glider flights at Netheravon Airfield, a Ministry of Defence grass strip airfield on Salisbury Plain, which he thoroughly enjoyed. "It was the first time I had flown," Harry says. "It was an exhilarating ride and the two pilots did us proud."

Two weeks later he was redeployed to the parachute training course. Needless to say, he passed the assessment process, including a medical examination and a series of demanding physical tests.

He revelled in the challenge of belonging to a regiment that was created with the express purpose of spearheading the Allies' return into Europe.

The trainee paratroopers took a train journey from Bulford to Chesterfield, 186 miles to the north, before marching 10 miles to Hardwick Hall, a magnificent Elizabethan house in Derbyshire, where they were housed on the extensive grounds in six-men bell tents. During the next few weeks they were subjected to arduous trials testing their physical and mental resilience, and were expected to live up to their motto 'Go to it!', espoused by their commander, Major-General Richard 'Windy' Gale.

The course at Hardwick Hall was make or break time for all aspiring paras. For 12 hours a day, from 7 am to 7 pm, all activity had to be completed 'at the double', with successive physical fitness instructors pushing the men to their limits. The challenges were daunting, including scaling 20-foot high scaffolds, crawling through flooded culverts, and negotiating trip wires and barbed wire on assault courses, in addition to unarmed combat, abseiling and cross-country running. The emphasis was on physical fitness, stamina and endurance.

The men were also ordered on gruelling route marches, wearing regulation uniforms including heavy boots, and carrying a hefty backpack. This was especially difficult when the weather was humid or rainy, as the wet uniforms chafed, especially on the shoulders, because of the straps on the backpacks. Army 'Ammo' boots, with iron toe and heel plates and hobnail-studded soles, played havoc with the men's feet, to the point of drawing blood, and long marches were always followed by a foot inspection.

Another demanding test for trainee paras, designed to instil combat skills, was termed milling, where two men of about the same size were each issued with a pair of boxing gloves and, for 60 long seconds, were required to "belt the daylights out of each other", wearing no protective gear. Harry's strategy was to go straight for his opponent's solar plexus, knocking the wind out of him before he could land the first punch – it worked every time!

On the Saturday of the first week of training Harry received word that his father was desperately ill, and he was granted nine days' compassionate leave. Sadly, following a relatively minor operation at age 48 and spending weeks in hospital, his father died the day after Harry arrived home, not knowing that he had joined the paras. At the time Harry's brother Wilf was a military captain serving in North Africa, his sister Lucy was serving in the Women's Auxiliary Air Force on a Bomber Command airfield, and his younger brother John was at school.

After the funeral, and helping his grieving mother, Harry returned to the unit, his future up in the air in more ways than one. Remarkably, leadership gave him the option of being back-squadded or continuing with his training but, true to form, he chose to continue. During the next few days the lack of exercise stretched his endurance to the limit, while the other trainees were riding the crest of a physical wave. Relying on his natural determination, and straining every nerve and muscle, Harry passed the course with flying colours.

On completion of the preliminary course the trainee paras speed-marched the 50 miles to RAF Ringway, now Manchester Airport, to begin their parachute training.

Before the men underwent their first test of parachuting, they were reasonably well conditioned to it, with initial training consisting of leaping out of a mock-up aircraft on the ground and learning how to safely fall. Despite this, there were some who at the point of jumping retreated, opting to return to their previous unit. This was permissible in training but after the coveted wings had been awarded anyone who refused to jump was court-martialled. The standard punishment was three months in a military gaol.

Harry's first two jumps were from a cage suspended from the base of an air raid defence barrage balloon, making a feet-first exit from a height of 850 feet before landing and rolling up his chute. "To be truthful," he says, "I didn't like the first jump and we had to do another that same evening." However, the high spirits of the other men, who were back-slapping each other and saying "How super!" spurred him on and he found his equilibrium on the second jump, which he quite enjoyed.

Before their first parachuting venture from a powered aircraft, the men were scheduled to be given an acclimatisation flight in an old converted Whitley bomber. However, due to an organisational irregularity, they were required to make a parachute jump on their first flight, which was not exactly to Harry's liking. A day or two later the men took off to have the acclimatisation flight they had missed earlier. Harry was to make eight more jumps – by this time "all good fun" for him – before qualifying for the coveted para wings.

After successfully completing the course at Ringway, the men were granted 14 days' leave before returning to Bulford. Harry was proud to become a fully-fledged member of J Section, the Signal Section of the 3rd Parachute Brigade, with the right-hand sleeve of his uniform now boasting the para wings between the Royal Signals flash at the shoulder seam and the Pegasus below. He also sported the famed red beret.

One of Harry's practice jumps during that time was on the day of a ceremonial visit from the Princess Royal, younger sister of King George VI, who was Colonel-in-Chief of the Royal Signals. The wind was extremely squally and normally practice jumps would have been cancelled but because the Colonel-in-Chief was in attendance the demonstration proceeded.

The 50 paras who took part endured the roughest of landings, being dragged along at a rate of knots until they were able to empty the air out of their chutes by frantically pulling on the lower rigging lines. Harry had an additional responsibility to contend with, as he had jumped with two canisters strapped to his chest, each containing a homing pigeon.

After the jump, Harry explained the role of the pigeons to the Princess – if for any reason the wireless sets didn't work the pigeons would do the job. Harry rolled up a message and placed it in a tiny tube which he clipped to a leg of one of the pigeons before launching it into the air. "The pigeons functioned well when they were released for the entertainment of our royal guest," Harry says.

When another royal visit took place a few weeks before D-Day Harry was quite taken with one of the party. “I first saw Princess Elizabeth in my military days,” he says. “King George VI and his wife Queen Elizabeth inspected the 3rd Parachute Brigade on a beautiful spring day, accompanied by Princess Elizabeth and a lady-in-waiting. The princess was beautifully dressed and looked absolutely charming.”

As D-Day neared, training ramped up and the paras made two jumps in four days. On the first jump Harry injured a knee and on the second he made it worse. But he was undeterred – had he not declined officer training to follow his dream? He concealed the extent of the injury because he had absolutely set his heart on being part of the D-Day landings.

Just three weeks after his 20th birthday, Signalman Harry Read of the 3rd Parachute Brigade, 6th Airborne Division Signals, was to endure the biggest challenge of his young life.

3

A LEAP OF FAITH

"It was a different world then. It was a world that required young men like myself to be prepared to die for a civilization that was worth living in."

~ HARRY READ

After months of intensive training, the paras were a crack team, poised to go into battle for King and country. The men of the 3rd Parachute Brigade assembled at RAF Down Ampney in Gloucestershire in preparation for D-Day, camping in bell tents at nearby Blakeneys Farm and attending strategic briefing sessions. For security reasons, no contact was allowed with the outside world.

The logistics of D-Day, code-named Operation Overlord, are mind-boggling; it was the largest naval, air and land operation in the history of warfare. The landing in Normandy, a region in north-western France with 350 miles of coastline on the English Channel, involved 156,000 Allied forces.

The briefing officers pulled no punches, informing the assembled paratroopers that they expected 50 per cent casualties on the D-Day landing alone, and declaring it was imperative that the objectives be achieved whatever the cost. The situation was critical, as the enemy was massing just 20 miles from England's shores. "Our plans are well-ordered," the officers added, "but when you land don't be surprised at the chaos."

Harry's reaction to hearing this grim news was to find a quiet place and try to get his head around the distinct possibility of losing his life. "All the natural feelings of immortality associated with young men disappeared for me," he says, "as, quite calmly, I faced the facts. My life was on the line for my country and I promised myself I would not shrink from doing whatever was required of me."

With D-Day scheduled for 5 June, it was planned that the paratroopers would fly out late at night on the 4th, dropping into Normandy by moonlight in the early hours of the morning on the day of the invasion. Their goal was to provide tactical support by taking over bridges and roads and securing the eastern flank of the Allied bridgehead. As the fateful day arrived, the paras steeled themselves for the coming conflict, only to be told that because of adverse weather conditions D-Day had been deferred for 24 hours.

Reveille sounded at 6 am the next morning, with a sergeant rallying the men to face what would prove to be the longest day of their young lives. For too many it would be their last. The weather had improved and it was all systems go for the D-Day landings. There was little time for idling, as the men double-checked their equipment and attended last-minute briefing sessions.

As night fell, Harry lined up with the men of 3rd Parachute Brigade to set out for RAF Down Ampney where they were met by an astonishing array of DC-3 Dakotas in take-off order. The paras' faces were camouflaged with black paint, and they were encouraged to put an extra hand grenade or two in their belts in addition to checking and rechecking the kitbags they had fastened to their right leg.

A poem Harry wrote many years later graphically describes the imminent challenges the paras were facing:

How vivid are those memories, dear Lord:
Our blackened faces, nervous, cheerful talk,
The parachutes, our laden, awkward walk,
With much equipment round our bodies stored.

The big occasion, yet not over-awed.
A motley group, not least the man from York,
From one another different – cheese from chalk.
A fearsome, though quite gentlemanly horde.

Within each heart a nagging, daunting fear:
Two hours from now and many will be dead
(Statistics make that brutal fact quite clear)
And some would fight like heroes born and bred.

Tensions were high as the men clambered into the aircraft, ready for take-off. Putting on a brave face, the paras engaged in their usual banter but the atmosphere became more and more sombre as the precariousness of their situation hit home. It was also anything but a direct flight – the aircraft cruised around again and again as part of a predetermined holding procedure and until every one of enormous number of planes was in formation the flight to Normandy would not begin.

Eventually the initial aircraft were on their way, with Harry and his mates among the first wave of paratroopers, bracing themselves for the coming challenge. They flew over the English Channel, catching glimpses of the ocean in the spasmodic moonlight, and all too soon approached their destination.

Harry describes the unforgettable moments before he exited the plane. "Ahead of us was what seemed to be a magnificent display of fireworks, with tracer bullets climbing lazily and gracefully into the sky. Slightly ahead of us an aircraft took a direct hit and plummeted to the ground. The anti-aircraft barrage was intense and we could hardly keep our seats. We were bouncing here, there and everywhere from the shockwaves from shells."

Then came their moment of truth as the aircraft slowed for the run-in to the drop zone at 0050 hours on the morning of D-Day, right on schedule. The red light came on and the men stood in line, facing the back of the aircraft. The plane was at 600 feet (to avoid attack during wartime, parachuting took place as close to the ground as possible) and the buffeting of the shells and the men's heavy loads made it difficult for them to keep their footing. Harry was para number 12 and, when the green light appeared, he shuffled in line to the exit, with an accumulator – a wireless battery the size and weight of a toolbox – strapped to his leg.

Adrenaline racing, he grabbed at the door frame to push off for the jump and was sent on his way by the dispatcher, "a big burly bloke" who assisted him out of the aircraft with a steadying and energetic hand. As he hit the night air of France he was rocked as never before by the slipstream, descending amid mortar fire and exploding shells. "You're at your most vulnerable as a para when you're hung by your shoulders," he says, "but surprisingly, although the activity was dangerous in the extreme, for those brief seconds I did not feel as vulnerable as I expected. It was unreal."

Thirty heart-stopping seconds later he landed. "But," he says, "it was a splash landing! We were on time but in the wrong place." Fortunately, he landed in waist-high water and the ground underneath was soft, so he was unhurt except for jarring his knee that had previously been injured in parachute training. There was no sign of any of his mates and no sign either of the bright green light which was to indicate the paras' rendezvous point.

In earlier briefings the men were informed that the dropping zone was between the Rivers Caen and Dives, and that, as an anti-parachute and glider deterrent, the enemy had dug substantial trenches in the low-lying land around the River Dives before flooding the area. Harry soon realised that he had landed east of the drop zone and he was in the flooded region. Completely alone, he looked up to see an Allied aircraft going down in flames.

After detaching himself from his 'chute and hoisting the heavy accumulator onto his shoulders, he began wading forward in the moonlight and suddenly plunged into a deep trench filled with water. Scrambling to extricate himself, he tugged on the surrounding grasses and weeds and pulled himself out. After retrieving the accumulator, he ventured a few yards further, only to tumble into yet another trench. When for a third time he disappeared underwater and struggled even harder to get out, he decided to discard the accumulator and tossed it back into the trench from which he had just emerged.

Sometime later, Harry spotted an indistinct figure in the watery distance. As he cautiously neared the man he was elated to recognise him as a member of the Brigade Headquarters Defence Platoon, known to him only as Paddy. Following procedure, the D-Day password 'ham and jam' was exchanged between the two. Harry reckons that, as the letter 'H' was not overused in the military, the resulting password of 'Ammonjam' had an Old Testament ring to it!

The pair made their way through a seemingly never-ending stretch of water, and as night turned to day there was still no land in sight. In the distance, they were troubled to see parachute canopies collapsed in silken circles on the water and sadly concluded that their fellow paras had been submerged in deep trenches on landing and had drowned, unable to free themselves from their heavy equipment.

Later Harry was to learn that only 15 per cent of paratroopers had landed in the planned zone, and as a result 192 men had died in flooded areas. In another tragic outcome, all but three of a further group of 43 paras were killed when one of the Allied bombers missed the designated target and hit their own men.

After an interminably long 16 hours of wading through frequently chest-high water while keeping up each other's spirits up, Harry and Paddy finally reached a patch of dry land late in the afternoon of D-Day. They took refuge on a knoll under a small cluster of trees, attempting to dry out in the afternoon sun, and had a meal from their emergency rations while keeping a nearby farmhouse under observation.

Assuming they were approaching the town of Robehomme, the two men cautiously made their way to the farmhouse at around 6 pm, and Paddy knocked on the door while Harry covered him with his Sten gun. The door opened and they were immediately invited inside, to the warmest of welcomes from the friendly farmer and his family, and a small group of paras who had already sought shelter and guidance there.

The English-speaking village priest, who was to become an indispensable ally, also welcomed them, warning them to stay in the farmhouse as there was danger all around, and promising to liaise with another group of paras who were holed up on the other side of Robehomme.

Forty tumultuous hours after the 6 am Reveille call on the previous day Harry fell into a fitful sleep in the adjoining barn. D-Day would be forever burned into his memory.

Early next morning the priest relayed the message that the men at the farmhouse would soon receive their instructions. Shortly afterwards, a sergeant arrived and ordered them to be ready to leave in a few hours. After a comparatively uneventful day, they were primed to go when he returned in the late afternoon to lead them the short distance to the other paras. From there the combined group would make their way to Le Mesnil, the site of the 3rd Parachute Brigade headquarters.

As night fell the men set off, venturing first through the German lines and then into the British lines – a hazardous journey during which they were frequently halted because of intermittent gunfire in the surrounding area. It was a long night. The men were reunited with their unit early on the morning of 8 June, two days after the parachute jump, and paras who hardly knew them greeted the arrivals like long-lost brothers.

"When we arrived, we realised how heavy our casualties had been," Harry says, "but with what remained of the brigade we continued with our own demanding, dangerous and costly service."

Harry was grieved to learn that Lance Corporal Josh Moore, a member of the Signals team and a good friend of his, was among the casualties, losing his life in action the day before. There were four in the radio team – the sergeant, corporal, lance corporal Josh and signalman Harry – and they were a tight-knit group. Josh was an achiever, always striving to be the best, and his loss was a real blow to Harry.

The Parachute Brigade Headquarters was set up on a large cheese farm, 100 yards from vital crossroads in the hamlet of Le Mesnil. Adjacent to the farmhouse was a dairy which was used by the medics attending to injured men, an adjoining barn became a mortuary and next to that was a smaller barn which became the signals office.

A few days after the men had settled themselves into their defensive position in order to secure the left flank of the invasion, their second-in-command was seriously wounded, leaving them under the care of the only sergeant who had survived the parachute drop.

A replacement officer was appointed, and the most senior Royal Signals officer at Divisional Headquarters accompanied him in order to introduce him to the section. On the way to their destination, a jeep carrying the men was targeted by the enemy, killing the lieutenant colonel, the captain and the driver.

Two representatives from each Signals section were assigned to attend their funeral, with the sergeant and Harry being chosen to represent their unit. Harry remembers that preparing for a funeral when stuck in trenches wasn't easy but they managed and duly attended. The burial place was a large field next to the local Catholic Church, which later became the Ranville War Cemetery. "The chaplain did his job well," Harry says, "and afterwards we returned to our work in the trenches."

While in the trenches, the men were given prepared rations and a limited amount of water, from which – in addition to drinking – they were required to wash and shave. Beards were not allowed but many of the men sported moustaches. "Cold water and a blunt razor blade constituted an attack on sensitive skin," Harry says. "Some of us, being very fair and very young, didn't have much to show but we were still ordered to go through the motions of having a shave!"

Harry remembers that the mixture of men in the paras was interesting. A small percentage had an inclination to violence which was legitimised by war, despite some of them having quite responsible jobs in 'civvy street'. A much larger percentage felt compelled to fight for their country, and preferred the challenge of the paras. Then there was a small band of dreamers – yearning for a world of peace and freedom – to which he belonged.

In order to defend the bridgehead, holding the position at Le Mesnil was crucial and their front line was under almost constant attack. At dawn and dusk each day every soldier had to man the trenches as these were the usual times for a concerted enemy assault. Sometimes the days seemed exceedingly long. "Survival wasn't the only goal but it was a relief to achieve it," Harry says.

After successfully holding their own at Le Mesnil, by the middle of August the 3rd Parachute Brigade went on the offensive and pursued the retreating German Army towards the River Seine. Harry, as the headquarters signals man, and his good friend Tony Bass, a medic, were at the front line of the breakout. Harry and Tony were kindred spirits and had resonated from their first meeting. "I thought he was a great man," Harry says. Because of his strong anti-war convictions Tony was a conscientious objector, opting to serve as a military combat medic in the paras.

With the enemy fighting a fierce rearguard action, the paras were under constant attack, and when a mortar shell exploded nearby a cry came out for the medics. "Tony grabbed his stretcher and with his long legs ran across the meadow. The remarkable thing was that whoever fired that mortar shell fired a second one that landed in precisely the same place and Tony was killed. It was devastating," Harry says.

It was from that experience, and the loss of other friends, that he later wrote the following verses:

Naught quietens more a former soldier's soul
Than looking at the headstones of his friends
Who fell in battle, striving for the goal
Of conquest, on which sacrifice depends.

Their loss was total – youth and love denied:
They lost their hopes, their dreams and undreamed dreams
That war's vile appetite be satisfied
And evil men fulfil their evil schemes.

While we, who by some chance evaded death
Look back on many crowded years of life,
Exhilarated by life's joy-filled breath
But saddened by these casualties of strife.

The headstones and the memories make me weep
For friends who in that cemetery sleep.

In Harry's words, he and his mates were "at the sharp end of one of the biggest and costliest battles of World War II". There were three distinct phases to the action he saw in Normandy. The first phase, from 6 June to 1 July, involved the invasion and securing the eastern flank of the beaches in order to block any enemy counter-offensive. As the paras dug in at Le Mesnil and held their line there were more casualties, but in the 12 days from 17 to 29 August, when in pursuit of the retreating enemy who fought an aggressive defensive action, the casualties were horrendous. In Harry's section alone, of the 100 men who made up the group, only 25 survived to return to England.

The commander of the 3rd Parachute Brigade, Brigadier James Hill, was to become one of the most highly decorated soldiers in the British Army, earning the Distinguished Service Order and two bars. In August, with the enemy withdrawing, Harry was one of two wireless operators assigned to man the roving radio set and accompany the brigadier on his rounds, either in a jeep or back-packing. As an HQ wireless operator he was often on the front line – sometimes in front of it – with Brigadier Hill. Harry deemed it an honour to serve under such a distinguished brigade commander.

One night, Brigadier Hill needed to communicate with a nearby battalion but their wireless set was not working, so he, his aide-de-camp and Harry, who was carrying a replacement wireless set, left the main group and set out on foot to make personal contact with them. When their progress was halted by enemy fire, they quickly moved off the road and the brigadier scanned a map by torchlight, looking for an alternative way. As mortar shells went screaming past, the three men hit the ground, with Harry's back taking the full force of the wireless set. After lying low for some time, the men regained their feet and pressed on.

Eventually linking up with the battalion, Harry handed over the replacement wireless set while the brigadier conferred with the leaders. On their return trek, a jeep jam-packed with men pulled up, seemingly from nowhere, and the brigadier, the ADC and Harry climbed aboard, hanging on for dear life as the jeep careered back to the main force.

On 7 September – three incredible, hazardous, costly and momentous months after D-Day – the 6th Airborne Division returned to the UK, sailing from the Mulberry B artificial harbour at Gold Beach Arromanches. According to official statistics published after the war, the 6000-plus men of the division suffered more than 4500 casualties.

Reflecting on those days, Harry says, "Some people think we felt the 'glory' of war, but I met only ordinary men who overcame their fears and pressed on to perform remarkable acts of bravery. One has only to stand by the graves of one's friends in a military cemetery to be unmanned by the cost. There is no glory in war and soldiers know that better than anyone else. When we consider the loss of life, friend or foe, from so many nations in World War II, we can only marvel at the level of sacrifice made by so many."

Other than the injury to his knee, however, Harry was not aware of suffering any ill-effects of battleground service. "There wasn't much about it to like and much about it that was horrendous," he says, "but the paras were all in it together. Though we had substantial casualties and challenges, all of that seemed to be bundled up in the essential experience of war." Their courage was not in vain, with D-Day being credited as the beginning of the end of World War II.

On his return to England, having been admitted to the Shaftesbury Military Hospital, the decision was made that Harry's injured knee – in spite of which he had soldiered on – would not stand up to the rigours of parachuting in the future and he was returned to unit.

"My problem was confirmed at the military hospital," Harry says, "but, because of the wide variety of knee injuries created by parachuting, the doctors chose not to operate, hoping that time might do what they felt they couldn't. My A1 medical grade was lowered to B7 which meant I had to return to an ordinary unit. My parachuting days were over." Or so he thought.

4

A HIGH CALLING

The greatness of a man's power is the measure of his surrender.

~ WILLIAM BOOTH

Stepping out on English soil again after three harrowing months on the battlefields of Normandy, Harry was quick to count his blessings. Although he was disappointed to be returned from the Parachute Brigade to the Royal Signals unit because of his knee injury, he looked to the future with great expectancy.

On being granted 10 days' leave, he journeyed to Grangetown to visit his mother and 11-year-old brother John, who both welcomed him with open arms. During that time his brother Wilf was serving as a captain in the Royal Artillery in North Africa, but Harry was able to visit his sister Lucy who was in a nearby hospital following a minor operation.

Returning from leave, he was sent to a troop holding camp at Thirsk in North Yorkshire. Still hoping for a return to the Parachute Brigade, and presuming there would be a ground job he could undertake with them, he approached the medical officer on a few occasions, only to be told each time that his medical records hadn't come through.

Eventually he was sent from Thirsk to undertake general duties at Scarborough, a town on England's North Sea Coast, one of his duties being to help prepare hotel accommodation for troops coming to the town. While something of an anti-climax to his time in Normandy, boredom was not in Harry's vocabulary, and he knuckled down to do his duty. During this time, with his spiritual wellbeing always at the back of his mind, he began to ask himself who he was and who he should be.

Late in the day of 7 May 1945, a few days before Harry's 21st birthday, it was announced on the radio that, after six long years of war, Germany had surrendered and the war had ended. The people were jubilant, with many dancing in the streets. Harry was more pensive, pondering about the sacrifice that so many, including his friends, had made in order to secure victory, and the millions on both sides who had died in the conflict. Victory in Europe, VE Day, was formally celebrated on 8 May.

After making a request to undertake military training as a driver with the Royal Signals unit, Harry was sent for a six-week driving course to Catterick, a large military camp not far from Grangetown. Having never driven a car before, he was a keen student, and thoroughly enjoyed the course. It was during this time that a momentous change took place in his life.

"During my military service, though I never became 'one of the boys', I lost the sharp edge of my faith," he says. "After some time I became convinced that I had life-changing decisions to make. It was at Catterick that I sought the Lord afresh, committed myself to him and applied to the Methodist Church to be a candidate for the ministry. My request was accepted and I began a study course in preparation for that.

"Having become properly saved I had no difficulty in witnessing to my mates," he continues. "Ex-paratroopers were allowed to wear their red berets and, of course, their wings, which probably meant that, in an ordinary unit, an ex-para was given a fair amount of respect, and I had no strong opposition to endure."

With a new lease on life and an extra spring in his step, after completing the driving course Harry was posted to the little town of Stromness in the Orkney Islands, off the north-eastern coast of Scotland. As the Orkneys share a similar latitude with Norway, the so-called land of the midnight sun, Harry was fascinated by the natural phenomenon of the seasons. "I thought it was fascinating to be outdoors during summer and be able to see and read at 1 o'clock in the morning," he says.

As well as undertaking driving duties for the Royal Signals at

Stromness, Harry was assigned to man the unit office. He undertook a secretarial training course, including learning to touch-type on an ancient manual typewriter, pecking away at the keys and listening for the bell that sounded at the end of each line. He was also allowed time to study for his post-military calling in the Methodist Church and, with the approval of his commanding officer, a Bible and other Christian study material sat on his desk.

As there was no Methodist Church in the town, Harry attended a small Mission Church each Sunday, where he learned of a weeknight Christian Servicemen's Fellowship. A couple of Salvationists in the fellowship told Harry of the Salvation Army corps in Kirkwall, some 12 miles away, adding that they had some difficulty in getting there. Because he was running the Signals office in addition to his driving duties, Harry gave himself permission to use the vehicle to take himself and the men to the Sunday meetings at Kirkwall.

An active and warm-hearted corps, Kirkwall had some long-established Salvation Army families and the men were blessed by the worship and fellowship, enjoying the distinctive dialect of the Orcadians. When the military facility in Stromness was closed due to demobilisation, they were sent to fulfil their duties in Kirkwall and Sunday meetings were within walking distance. Eventually the camp at Kirkwall was also closed and Harry was assigned to the beautiful city of Edinburgh, albeit reluctant to leave the corps where strong friendships had been made.

On being posted to Edinburgh and continuing his studies towards the Methodist ministry, Harry came under the care of the minister at the Methodist Central Hall in Tollcross, south-west of the city centre. A former Oxford rowing blue, the minister was welcoming without being, in Harry's words, "unduly fulsome", and Harry attended the Methodist church each Sunday.

When Saturday nights came around, Harry chose not to accompany the other Signals men to the cinema or the pub, and the only church that advertised a Saturday night meeting in the local newspaper was The Salvation Army. He regularly attended the praise meeting on Saturday evenings at the Edinburgh Gorgie Corps and, although they knew he was working toward the Methodist ministry, he was made more than welcome.

When the officer at the corps told him of special meetings being held in Glasgow, suggesting that he might enjoy them, Harry took a weekend pass so he could attend. That seemingly insignificant choice would change his life, as it was during those meetings he realised that God was compellingly and unmistakably calling him to officership in The Salvation Army.

"God's guidance was clear and sure," he says. "Having been born into a Salvation Army family I was to accept my heritage and become a Salvation Army officer. To this guidance I was totally obedient if not overly enthusiastic at the time," he adds frankly, "but from that obedience flowed joy and pride in Jesus Christ, and a lifetime of total fulfilment."

He arranged an interview with the Methodist minister to share his decision and, understandably, the minister was not overly impressed. So it was in June 1946 that, at the age of 22, Harry became a soldier of The Salvation Army at the Edinburgh Gorgie Corps, solemnly signing the Articles of War as he was sworn in wearing military uniform.

From that time on Harry became a stalwart soldier of the corps, and the Salvationists were delighted to learn of his decision to become an officer. After making an application to become a candidate, Harry was interviewed by the candidates secretary and the divisional commander, who were both warm and encouraging. The divisional commander recommended that Harry attend the Thursday night central holiness meeting in Edinburgh, which he was more than happy to do.

A missionary officer, Major (Dr) William McAllister, who was on homeland leave, told Harry that Major Frederick Coutts, who was at that time serving in the Editorial Department at International Headquarters, would be speaking at an upcoming bandsmen's and songsters councils in Edinburgh and suggested Harry attend. After the Saturday night meeting in which Frederick Coutts spoke, Harry got on a crowded bus to head back to military camp and had just sat down when Major McAllister and Major Coutts boarded the bus. "Please, take my seat," Harry said. In his military uniform, he was introduced to Frederick Coutts and they shook hands, not knowing that this brief meeting was the prelude to a lifelong friendship.

At that time Harry had served for six years in the military, including his time in the Air Defence Cadet Corps and the Home Guard, and was due to be demobilised the following year. He informed his military superior officers of his plans to become a Salvation Army officer and was allowed to use the office in which he worked during the day as a study room in the evenings.

One evening the door opened and Bill Day, a corporal who he knew fairly well, came into the office to check things out. Harry was typing a short talk he was to give at the corps the next Sunday and the corporal stood behind him, reading over his shoulder. As he discussed with Harry the content of talk, after many questions and much earnest discussion, Harry suggested that perhaps he should do something about his need for God.

"The result was that we knelt at the office desk and I led my friend to the Lord – the very first person I had ever led to salvation. The sheer joy and exultation of leading someone to the Lord is one of the deepest spiritual experiences one can experience. Though all subsequent experiences are wonderful, there can only ever be a first, and Bill Day was that for me."

Bill told one or two of his close friends about what had happened and it became common knowledge in the Signals camp. He accompanied Harry each Sunday to Edinburgh Gorgie Corps and became part of the warm Salvation Army fellowship there. While the young people's sergeant major and his wife invited Harry to their home for meals on Sundays, the corps sergeant major and his wife did the same for Bill.

At the conclusion of seven years' military service, Harry was demobilised in June 1947 and entered the King's Messengers session at the William Booth Memorial International Training College in August of that year. Along with three others, he farewelled from Grangetown Corps, with his proud mother and brother John in the congregation among the Salvationists his family had enjoyed fellowship with for many years.

Suitcases in hand and full of youthful exuberance, the four Grangetown recruits arrived at the entrance of the International Training College in Denmark Hill, ready to face the challenges of the next nine months. Opened in 1929 by Prince George, Duke of Kent, the college had replaced the International Training Garrison at Clapton, and the imposing building has since become a London landmark.

The 250 cadets of the 1947-48 King's Messengers session, including men and women from Norway, Sweden, Denmark, Holland, France, Italy, Chile, Rhodesia and the British Territory, were welcomed in the college's assembly hall, with Harry wearing Salvation Army uniform for the first time. Commissioner John Bladin, the training commissioner, introduced the cadets to the chief side officer for men, Lieut-Colonel William Cooper, and the chief side officer for women, Colonel Anna Sowton.

Harry came to have a high regard for the college staff, some of whom had served in the Forces, and others who had tended to those suffering the effects of the World War II conflict during bombings, bereavements and life in the underground shelters. Among those he had great admiration for were Lieut-Colonel William Cooper, a square-jawed man who had served in the Navy in minesweepers in World War I; Adjutant Geoffrey Dalziel, who inspired Harry with his spirituality and drive; and Adjutant Harry Dean, a brilliant thinker and communicator. "Male and female Salvation Army officers alike were heroic in their service and commitment at the Training College," Harry says.

As for the cadets' training regime, it was specified as follows: "The intensive Training College curriculum is intended to train cadets to become Salvation Army officers strong in character and zealous for the saving of souls, and includes lessons and lectures on scripture, Army history and discipline, and the preparation of addresses. Periods spent at corps and other centres of work in London, with occasional campaigns further afield, will give practical insight into Salvation Army activities. Courses of first aid will prepare cadets for the various emergencies which all officers are called to face."

The college was segregated, with separate quarters, dining rooms and evangelical activities for male and female cadets. Most of the training programme took place in all-session groups and class teaching, with separate seating arrangements for men and women.

The discipline of training for one army meant that Harry had no difficulty in training for another and he readily accepted the rigours of Training College life. It was noted by leadership that those men and women cadets who had recently been released from military service showed marked development following their experiences in the Forces. As for Harry, being the only ex-paratrooper in the session – and in fact the only World War II para to ever become a Salvation Army officer – he enjoyed "a fair amount of credibility".

If Harry had one reservation about the training curriculum it was from time to time about the lectures. The staff, he says, were wonderful but when it came to the educational programme some aspects had been carried over from the 1930s, with tutors obliged to follow notes provided by the college's education department. With his analytical mindset, Harry felt some of the lectures needed updating, and he often asked questions to clarify current issues.

The evangelical aspect of the training programme was well to the fore. Harry was involved in cadets' open air meetings at well-known London locations such as Leicester Square and Hyde Park, and engaged in personal contact with interested onlookers. He also participated in practical field training, including campaigns at corps and other Salvation Army centres of work in London.

Also on the cadets' agenda was door-knocking for the annual Self Denial Appeal. One afternoon when Harry asked a rather well-spoken man for a donation his response was, "Indeed, I will not donate – you killed Bramwell!" He was, of course, referring to the events of 1929 in which The Salvation Army High Council voted 55 to 8 to remove 73-year-old General Bramwell Booth from office due to his inability to continue because of illness. "In 1929 I was but five years old, but I suppose I'm guilty by association," Harry says with a smile.

Academic pursuits at the college took precedence and there was an extensive reading list for the cadets. However, Harry says, the book that gave his life spiritual wings was titled *A Testament of Devotion*, written by Quaker teacher Thomas R. Kelly. Harry was loaned the book by the secretary to the training principal – "a very informed, gracious lady" – and he copied out in a notebook profound passages that spoke to his heart, including the following:

"I have in mind something deeper than the simplification of our external programs, our absurdly crowded calendars of appointments through which so many pantingly and frantically grasp… There is a deeper, an internal simplification of the whole of one's personality, stilled, tranquil, in childlike trust listening ever to Eternity's whisper, walking with a smile into the dark."

Harry also admired many Salvation Army heroes of the faith, whose courage and faithfulness moved him deeply. They included Commissioner Frederick Booth-Tucker, an exemplar of incarnational ministry in India; Captain (later Lieut-Colonel) Harry Andrews, The Salvation Army's first medical man in India, who was made an MBE in 1918 and posthumously awarded the Victoria Cross; and Commissioner Herbert Lord, OBE, a pioneer officer in Korea, whose faith never faltered, despite horrific experiences of being a prisoner of war in Changi, and some years later being forced to take part in the infamous death march in Korea.

During this time The Salvation Army's International Headquarters was housed at the Training College after being totally destroyed in an air raid during World War II, and one of the highlights for Harry were the visits to the cadets and staff by General Albert Orsborn. As General, he visited and ministered on five continents. Known as 'the Poet-General of The Salvation Army', General Orsborn was a prolific songwriter and many of his inspirational songs are included in The Salvation Army song book.

Another of the highlights of Harry's time in training were the spiritual days held at the college. He has an enduring memory of General Orsborn speaking to the cadets on one such occasion. "I had such respect for him," Harry says. "He was a brilliant speaker and an inspiring meeting leader, with a resonant voice and a wonderful presence."

Harry also admired General Orsborn's talent as a poet – Albert Orsborn's first book, a collection of verses titled *The Beauty of Jesus: Selected Songs and Poems*, was published in 1947. The art of poetry had captivated Harry from his schooldays when he memorised numerous verses of favourite poets, in addition to writing humorous rhymes for his friends to chortle at. Experiences at the Training College rekindled his poetic leanings, and he began to actively pursue his aptitude.

Harry shared a couple of his poems with a cadet friend and, unbeknown to him, his friend passed them on to a college staff member, who sent for Harry and told him he should talk to Lieut-Colonel Catherine Baird of the International Headquarters Literary Department, which was at that time housed at the Training College. Catherine Baird was a poet, editor and writer who had been encouraged in her writing by Commissioner Samuel Logan Brengle, a revered author and preacher on the doctrine of holiness. In mentoring Catherine Baird, Commissioner Brengle sparked what he vividly described as her "pen of flame".

Lieut-Colonel Baird graciously received Harry and assessed his poems. She gently advised him that he was trying to accomplish too much in one set of verses – her guidance was to focus on one major thought and develop it to a powerful conclusion. Harry revised his poem two or three times before she was satisfied. He was honoured when Lieut-Colonel Baird published his poem in *The Warrior*, one of the Salvation Army young people's publications she edited, in addition to being the editor of *The Young Soldier*. She also gave him a book on the basic technicalities of poetry, songs and hymns, which he carefully studied.

"My close contacts with Colonel Baird through the following years influenced not only my writing, but my entire life," Harry says. "I thought then, and think still, that she was one of the most remarkable of our women officers. What a wonderful woman! What a marvellous example of Christlikeness! I can only think of superlatives and she merits every one of them. Her verses and influence will live forever."

The nine months of Training College life – so pivotal to his future as a Salvation Army officer – passed quickly for Harry. He thoroughly enjoyed the camaraderie and fellowship of the college staff and fellow cadets. He also relished the challenge of college discipline and the rigorous training, including early-morning prayer meetings, Bible studies, lectures, examinations, open-air evangelism, soul-winning, social service experiences and compulsory physical exercise – not to mention the cadets' obligatory polishing, scrubbing and dusting of the college interior.

The cadets' covenant day preceding their commissioning as officers of The Salvation Army was held at the Training College on Thursday 4 May 1948, led by the Chief of the Staff, Commissioner John Allen. In a sanctified spirit of dedication, one by one the cadets knelt at the place of prayer to sign their sacred covenant with God.

Having confirmed their calling, Cadet Harry Read and the more than 200 men and women cadets of the King's Messengers session prepared with a mix of excitement and anticipation for their upcoming commissioning services, to be held in London's famed Royal Albert Hall.

5

UNDER HIS WINGS

"For I know the plans I have for you," declares the Lord,
"plans to prosper you ... plans to give you hope and a future."
~ JEREMIAH 29:11

The Kensington Gardens environs of the Royal Albert Hall were thronged with Salvationists on Friday 14 May 1948, prior to the commissioning services of the King's Messengers session of cadets. The afternoon and evening events were a sell-out, with a capacity crowd in the 5000-plus seats on the floor of the hall and in the upper tiers.

The spectacular glass-domed venue of the Royal Albert Hall added to the pageantry and sense of occasion as, following the sessional flag and with heads held high, the cadets marched down the aisles and onto the platform to the strains of the International Staff Band, with Commissioner John Bladin, the training commissioner, taking the salute.

The commissioning and appointments meeting was held in the afternoon, and there was a sense of celebration and high excitement as the newly-commissioned lieutenants received their first appointments. The huge crowd listened with keen interest as each appointment was announced, not least Harry's family and his mother Florence, who was later to become a proud recipient of the Order of the Silver Star, presented to mothers of graduating cadets.

As Harry stepped up to receive his appointment, he was greeted with the words: "Harry Read, you are appointed as the young people's sergeant at the International Training College," an announcement that did not come as a surprise to him.

In a short meeting at the Training College, on the morning

of the commissioning events, Commissioner Bladin gave a special word of thanks to the cadet sergeants of the King's Messengers session before announcing the names of the sergeants for the incoming Peacemakers session. Although Harry was looking forward to the challenge of being appointed to a corps, he felt honoured to have been selected as one of the nine cadet sergeants for the men's side, as had his good friend Ken Lawson.

The dedication meeting for the King's Messengers took place in the evening, beginning with a pageant titled 'Go Swift Messengers', in which most of the cadets took part. Tracing messengers through the scriptures, the various scenes depicted them being awakened, called, frustrated and vindicated. The climax of the pageant came when the flags of every session of cadets at the International Training College since its inception at Denmark Hill in 1929 were brought to the platform, followed by the flag of the King's Messengers session.

The pageant was followed by the dedication of the lieutenants, a solemn and sacred occasion as they publicly affirmed their calling and promised to devote their lives to serving God and The Salvation Army. As Harry reflected on his calling he felt God's presence very near.

The commissioning meetings continued over the weekend, with a farewell festival held on Saturday night in the Westminster Central Hall, a venue with a seating capacity of 2300. It was a joyous and uplifting occasion, including special presentations by the new lieutenants in celebration of their service as the King's Messengers.

Sunday was the culmination of the commissioning weekend, with farewell meetings held in the capacious Camberwell Citadel which was packed to the rafters by the huge congregation, including Harry's family. The cadets marched down Denmark Hill from the nearby Training College and held an open air meeting in an adjacent street before filing in for the holiness meeting. It was a busy and God-honouring day, with a praise meeting in the afternoon followed by the salvation meeting at 7 pm.

On the Thursday morning following commissioning, the new

lieutenants, with hearty farewells and the prayers of staff ringing in their ears, caught trains or buses en route to their appointments. As for Harry, after the departing lieutenants had been given a rousing send-off, he and the other cadet sergeants were soon busily engaged in preparing their programmes for the incoming cadets. Another of their duties was to clean and ready the college for the arrival of the 235 cadets of the Peacemakers session and, in Harry's words, the young sergeants took to scrubbing floors "with a light heart".

Both male and female sergeants worked under the direction of their sectional officer and lived at the Training College on the same floor as the cadets in their brigade. As young people's sergeant, however, Harry did not have oversight of a cadet brigade but was appointed to train each of the male cadets in working with children and young people. He gave tutorials at the college and also accompanied groups of cadets to corps to engage with young people and take part in street evangelism.

"I didn't live in the same conditions as the other sergeants," Harry says, "because they were closely linked with their brigades. As there was no sergeant for the married cadets, I lived on the same floor as a number of married couples. Some of the ladies took me to heart and offered to do my cleaning. The friendships made in those days lasted for a lifetime."

Major Frederick Coutts at that time was a member of the International Headquarters Literary Department, having spent 11 years preparing weekly scripture reading material for The Salvation Army's youth and children's work and study material for corps cadets. As editor of *The Officers' Review*, he visited the college one evening to speak to a group of cadets who were Harry's responsibility as young people's sergeant.

The cadets had an evening meal together, pushed their chairs back and listened with great interest to the guest speaker. Afterwards, Harry chatted with Major Coutts, and during their conversation asked, "And how is Major McAllister?" The major paused, thought for a few moments and then said to Harry, "We met on that bus in Edinburgh, didn't we?" Although quite some time had passed since Harry had replaced his military khaki with the navy blue serge of a Salvation Army uniform, to his surprise Frederick Coutts recalled their chance meeting in Edinburgh.

Knowing of Harry's interest in writing, Major Coutts sent him a recommended book from time to time, and frequently checked on what he was reading. In one of their conversations Major Coutts, who was to become the author of 11 books during his lifetime, spoke of his writing discipline and how he would write and rewrite again and again, until he knew he could do no better. "Ever since that time I've tended to follow his example," Harry says.

He continued to look forward to the visits to the Training College of General Albert Orsborn after returning from his extensive overseas travels. The General wanted to "give the Army wings", travelling by air more than 350,000 miles in eight years to strengthen The Salvation Army's international fellowship after World War II.

"As a young cadet sergeant on the Training College staff," Harry says, "I recall how we gathered to welcome General Orsborn back from his many travels across the world. He never referred to the unsafe nature of travelling in faraway places – unsafe roads, railways, boats, towns and villages – but only to preserving our internationalism, and nurturing and encouraging those fellow Salvationists who are permanently resident in places of challenge and danger, albeit places of great spiritual victories."

Life for Harry as young people's sergeant was busy and fulfilling. As well as the supervision and mentoring of cadets in their preparation for working with young people, he was also involved in mandatory post-appointment studies and classes held for the 19 male and female sergeants at the college. As cadet sergeants, both men and women attended the tutorials, and there was a fair amount of banter, Harry says, as they were not regimented in the same way as the cadets.

One night a birthday party was held for one of the cadets at her parents' home and during the evening Harry spoke for the first time to a fellow cadet sergeant, Winifred Humphries. "I've always looked a bit younger than my years," Harry says, "and Win thought when we met on that occasion that I was one of the 18-year-olds, whereas I was actually the ripe old age of 23. That was our first association; I thought she was lovely, intelligent and personable."

With the female sergeants' mess and the male sergeants' mess on the same floor, there was plenty of opportunity for friendly conversation and Harry became increasingly drawn to Sergeant Humphries.

Later he was to discover that Winifred Humphries was born to staunch Salvationist parents in Mexborough, South Yorkshire. An only child, she attended the Mexborough Grammar School where she excelled in her studies and was nominated to go to university, but chose instead to attend teachers college. Following her graduation, she taught at a school in Rotherham, not far from Mexborough, and was soon appointed as the deputy headmistress. It was at this time that the Lord put his hand on Win and called her to serve as a Salvation Army officer.

After prayerful consideration, Harry decided to talk to his chief side officer, Lieut-Colonel Will Cooper, about his feelings for Win. The protocol in those days was that if cadet sergeants felt an affinity with someone, with a view to eventual marriage, they were obliged to advise their senior officer that they had 'an interest' in that person. So Harry spoke to Will Cooper and told him of his attraction to Cadet Sergeant Humphries. "Does she have feelings for you?" Will asked, to which Harry answered, "I haven't spoken with her about it."

Colonel Cooper immediately phoned his counterpart, Colonel Anna Sowton, to inform her of his conversation with Harry and enquire whether she'd had a similar chat with Winifred Humphries. "Actually, Sergeant Humphries hasn't mentioned it," she said.

The colonels' conversation then turned to an upcoming conference, to be held at the Army's Sunbury Court Conference Centre, regarding an innovative scheme targeting young people attending university or college. As the Training College was required to send two delegates to this event, Will Cooper asked Anna Sowton who she was sending as her representative, to which she answered,

"I'm sending Cadet Sergeant Humphries." Will Cooper promptly replied, "And I'm sending Cadet Sergeant Harry Read."

Harry and Win travelled by public transport to the conference centre and sat together during proceedings in the massive, high-ceilinged conference room of the west wing. From that day on, with the blessing of their senior officers, romance blossomed for the young couple. "Win was hugely gifted and deeply spiritual," Harry says. "Together we helped nourish and shape each other into what we were to become."

For the cadet sergeants, the busy, productive nine months of caring for and nurturing the cadets of the Peacemakers session were coming to an end, and preparations began for the commissioning of the 1948-49 intake of cadets, to be held in the Royal Albert Hall on the second Friday in May.

Harry and Win and, of course, the other cadet sergeants had a keen interest in their own appointments – to be announced along with those of the new lieutenants in the afternoon meeting – as did both of their families, who were part of the huge congregation. They were soon to find out.

Bright-eyed with anticipation, when Harry stepped up and stood in line to receive his appointment he was introduced by Major Harry Warren, the field training officer, as Cadet Sergeant Henry Read. Henry Read? Harry smiled, while his family and friends looked at each other in surprise. "Cadet Sergeant Harry Read," said Commissioner Bladin, "you are appointed in charge of the Dorking Corps with the rank of lieutenant."

In conversation with Major Warren later, Harry said, "Do you mind me saying I'm not Henry Read? I'm Harry Read." The major immediately apologised, explaining that although his own name was officially Henry he was more often than not called Harry.

And what of Win? Lieutenant Winifred Humphries was appointed to Hedge End Corps in Hampshire. Harry and Win were more than happy to discover that Hedge End, a town not far from Southampton, was easily accessible by train from Dorking.

Following the commissioning weekend, Harry and Win said

their fond farewells and took leave of their leaders and college comrades of the past nine months before boarding trains to their respective destinations. Travelling with Harry to Dorking, a market town in central Surrey in south-east England, about 21 miles south of London, was Lieutenant Ted Cotterill, who had also been appointed to the corps. They went with much anticipation and high hopes.

On arrival at Dorking railway station, Harry and Ted were welcomed by two soldiers of the corps, a policeman and his wife, who escorted them to their quarters at 4 Harrowgate Gardens. They walked up the path to the entrance, to find their accommodation was one of a group of four apartments at the address, with a small living room, an even smaller kitchen and two upstairs bedrooms, not to mention an outside toilet in a shed. In spite of its impressive address, the apartment was rather primitive, Harry says, but they had no complaints.

As for housekeeping, the two young officers fended for themselves, coping with cooking, cleaning, laundry, and shopping at the town centre that was within walking distance from their quarters. Without a car, their corps visitation was done by bicycle, bus or train.

Rather than cooking a main meal for themselves, they often visited the local British Restaurant, one of many across the country that had been set up by the government to combat the severity of rationing which had continued after World War II. The restaurants were staffed by members of the Women's Voluntary Services, with a typical meal consisting of roast beef, roast potatoes, peas, gooseberry tart and custard, plus a cup of tea. Harry and Ted were more than happy to pay ninepence each for this hearty meal.

The first few months were a steep learning curve for the two young lieutenants as they settled into life as corps officers. Dorking was a small corps that had been at the point of closing a few years earlier but Harry was to discover that the preceding officer, Lieutenant Bramwell Prince, had a powerful ministry and during his time the congregation prospered. Once again there was a band

and songster brigade, Sunday school, corps cadets and home league.

Life was demanding and productive – leading meetings, preparing sermons, getting to know their congregation, oversighting the various corps activities, visiting pubs selling *The War Cry*, organising the corps finances and liaising with Divisional Headquarters.

Three months into their appointment, a further challenge confronted Harry when his associate and friend Lieutenant Ted Cotterill was required to move, supposedly for two weeks, because of a breakdown elsewhere.

"Ted never returned," Harry says. "That first night when he had gone, as I knelt to say my prayers I felt very lonely. But the Lord seemed to be saying, 'Harry, there are some things I can only do for you when you're alone.' I've transposed that insight into every difficult, testing situation since."

Shouldering the additional responsibility, and with much prayer and preparation, Harry applied himself to sole leadership of the corps, including three open airs and three meetings on Sunday, frequent visitation of corps members, and becoming the face of The Salvation Army in the Dorking community.

In the early days of his officership he realised he had the gift of encouragement, and that became a major factor in his service through the years. "In my ministry I affirm people, gently challenge them to live up to their potential and give as much support as I can for them to live the life of faith."

While there were never quite enough hours in the day for Harry as he dedicated himself to the demands of his calling, Win was never far from his mind. She had settled in and was enjoying leadership of the Hedge End Corps along with the second officer, Lieutenant Peggy Nobbs, who became a lifelong friend.

Communication between Harry and Win was less than they would have wished. Newly-commissioned officers' quarters did not generally have telephones so they pre-arranged a time for their weekly phone call from a local public telephone box, hoping that at that time it would not be already occupied.

As for face-to-face meetings, the so-called 'courting' regulation was that they could meet only once a month, and they counted the days until they could see each other again. When the time came, Harry took a two-hour train journey from Dorking, and Win made the 40-minute trip from Hedge End, before meeting at Southsea railway station and spending the day together. Very soon they were making plans for their wedding.

Some time before the wedding, however, Win's father George, with whom she enjoyed a deep and loving relationship, became seriously ill and Win was granted permission to return home to help her mother Ivy, who was also not well, look after her father. During World War I, after enlisting when he had just turned 17 ('misrecalling' his age to the recruiting officers), George eventually became a sergeant in the Royal Naval Division. He served in Belgium and France as well as at Gallipoli, and fought on the front line at the Siege of Antwerp, the Somme, Paschendael and other major battles until he was injured during the German Spring Offensive in 1917.

On his return he became a miner and was seriously injured in an underground rock fall, from which he never fully recovered. Sadly, George died six weeks before Win and Harry's wedding. After some discussion about postponing the wedding, it was decided to proceed.

So it was that in the afternoon of a late spring day, Saturday 28 May 1950, at Mexborough, Win's home corps, she and Harry were married. Delighted family, friends and comrades filled the hall, and the ceremony was conducted by Commissioner John Bladin, the training commissioner, who had earlier confided in Win that he would be happy to officiate on this special occasion.

In full Salvation Army uniform, and attended by Harry's friend Bill McGowan, Win's friend Nellie Harding and flower girl Pat Norman, Harry and Win exchanged their vows, pledging their lifelong love for each other. Wedding photos show the absolute delight of the happy couple.

Harry's lyrical poem, written some years later, beautifully describes their joy:

Love is sweet tranquillity:
Birds soaring gracefully;
Breezes lazing on the sea;
Country sounds and country fragrance;
Tender music, gentle cadence;
Peace invading every sense,
Love is sweet tranquillity.

Love is all activity:
Verbs jostling eagerly,
Full of joyful energy.
The verb to trust, the verb to care,
The verb to have, the verb to share,
The verb to hold, the verb forbear.
Love is all activity.

Love is for eternity:
Moments speeding stealthily
Cannot slow the alchemy
Of love, becoming much more precious,
To man and wife who vow 'to cherish' –
And God himself makes that love glorious.
Love is for eternity.

After a brief, idyllic one-week honeymoon, staying at a beautiful house in Plymouth loaned to them by Harry's brother Wilf, the newlyweds journeyed to their first corps appointment as a married couple.

6

LEADING THE WAY

If your actions inspire others to dream more, learn more and become more, you are a leader.
~ JOHN QUINCY ADAMS

A few weeks before their marriage, Harry and Win received word that they were to be appointed to Chichester Corps on the south coast of West Sussex. Although they had mixed feelings about leaving their first appointments after just one fruitful year as corps officers, they looked forward to service as a married couple in this historic city. Chichester is known for its iconic cathedral, with its soaring spire dominating the skyline for miles around.

As the official date for the beginning of their service at Chichester was 18 May 1950, ten days before their wedding, Harry arrived to take charge of the corps two weeks beforehand. After receiving a rousing and affectionate farewell from comrades and friends at Dorking on his last Sunday there, the following Thursday a married couple from the corps kindly took him by car to Chichester.

He was welcomed by the Chichester corps treasurer, Mrs Tamplin, who took him to the officers' quarters, situated in a row of terrace houses not far from the city. Similar to his previous quarters at Dorking, the premises were small but adequate, with the passageway leading to a small living room, dining room, and a kitchen with a large stone-built, fire-powered boiler. Harry went upstairs and quickly unpacked his few possessions before preparing to meet his Chichester comrades.

The welcome meeting at the corps that evening was led by Brigadier John Nicholson, the divisional chancellor. The well-attended gathering included comrades and friends of the Chichester Corps and also quite a few less-regular attenders who had decided to check out the new corps officer.

The very next morning Harry was inspired to make a visit to those listed in the corps visitation book. They were surprised and delighted to receive a personal call from their corps officer so soon after his arrival. Harry's pastoral care was to reap huge benefits.

"Preparing for the Sunday meeting was no problem," he says. "The congregation was warm and welcoming, including those people who for one reason or another had distanced themselves from the corps, some of whom I had visited on the Friday, and the mercy seat appeal was quite wonderful."

When Lieutenant Harry and Mrs Lieutenant Win Read arrived at the corps as newlyweds after their short honeymoon, members of the congregation immediately took them to their hearts. Harry and Win enjoyed sharing leadership of the corps and their combined talents complemented each other in a successful and effective partnership. Harry says, "I had to be a good steward of Win's gifts. Win could do just about anything and do it better than most other people. Had she not married she could have been a distinguished leader in her own right."

So the corps prospered and was warmly accepted by the local community. Outreach and open airs were held regularly in the vicinity and, Harry says, Chichester Corps was buzzing with activity and personal evangelism. The public was also generous when giving to the Self Denial and Harvest Appeals. As far as personal income was concerned, however, Harry and Win often had to keep in mind the old saying: "You should not mind living from hand to mouth, so long as it is God's hand and your mouth."

"Win and I became officers in the days when all the bills of the corps had to be paid first," Harry says, "and if there wasn't enough left to meet the officers' allowance that was just unfortunate. We were grateful to belong to Army families who were very helpful.

"It's true, sacrifice was involved in those early days but it was a privilege to be called to officership and the personal satisfactions far outweighed concerns about income. Everything depended upon the strength of the call to officership. If you were sure it was of God then you soldiered on with obedience, initiative and joy. It certainly worked well in our case. It was on that kind of sacrifice that the foundations of the Army we know and love were laid."

Soon after settling in at the corps, Harry and Win endeared themselves to the wider Chichester community, including the Bishop of Chichester Cathedral, George Bell, who became a good friend of The Salvation Army. An Anglican theologian, Dean of Canterbury, a member of the House of Lords and a pioneer of the ecumenical movement, the Bishop was one of the truly great church leaders of his day. After each visit to Bishop Bell, Harry was blessed by the farewell message on the wall of the Cathedral: "We wish you good luck in the Name of the Lord" (Psalm 129 verse 8 in the Common Prayer Translation).

Harry was invited to speak to students of the various schools in the area, including the local Catholic schools, about The Salvation Army and its place in the Church. "I always got a good hearing from the interested students," Harry says, "William and Catherine Booths' spiritual emphasis and evangelistic success ensured that."

During their time at Chichester, Harry and Win were overjoyed when it was confirmed by the local doctor that they were expecting their first child. The comrades of the corps shared their joy and some of the home league ladies set to work knitting baby clothes while they looked forward to greeting the new arrival. However, welcoming the new baby to Chichester was not to be.

When Harry advised Divisional Headquarters of Win's pregnancy, the divisional commander, Lieut-Colonel Herbert Murray and his wife, a kind and caring couple who were always aware of the wellbeing of their officers, sent their congratulations and best wishes. More than that, when on making enquiries they found that the childbirth facilities at Eastbourne were superior to those at Chichester, it was decided that Harry and Win would be transferred to Eastbourne Old Town Corps at the next field change.

Taking a well-earned break on furlough, Harry and Win first stayed with Win's mother at Mexborough who was, of course, delighted to see them. They then journeyed to Plymouth, where Harry's older brother Wilf and his wife Rose lived with their family. Concerned that his mother Florence, widowed since 1943 and still living in Grangetown, Yorkshire, was unwell, Wilf organised the rental of a house near where he and Rose lived, for his mother and younger brother John. Harry and Win stayed with Florence and John, and saw a great deal of Wilf and Rose. It was a joyous time.

Refreshed and revitalised, Harry and Win returned to Chichester, continuing to partner with the corps in worship and outreach to the community. All too soon, after 12 blessed and rewarding months at Chichester, they were farewelled to Eastbourne Old Town, arriving there just a few weeks before the baby's birth.

Eastbourne, a town on the south-east coast in East Sussex, 70 miles south of London, is located on England's so-called Sunshine Coast, with spectacular views over the English Channel from the chalk cliffs of Beachy Head. Eastbourne's oldest neighbourhood, Eastbourne Old Town, is just 1.7 miles away from Eastbourne proper. As its name suggests, it is home to many historic landmarks, including a 12th century pub and St Mary's, Eastbourne's parish church for almost 1000 years.

Harry and Win were greeted at Eastbourne Old Town in a spirit of joy. Looking to the future, the corps comrades and friends gave Harry and Win, who was at this stage heavily pregnant, a welcome to be remembered. There were two Salvation Army corps in the vicinity, Eastbourne and Eastbourne Old Town, and they co-existed in a spirit of conviviality and cooperation.

Eastbourne Citadel was a large corps that had a long and colourful history. In the 1890s persecution of The Salvation Army in the area was so strong that a bylaw was passed making it illegal for the Army to hold outdoor gatherings. The Salvationists defied the ban, much to the anger of locals who formed a 'skeleton army', attacking them and destroying their instruments. Undaunted, the corps continued its soul-saving calling, and six decades later was alive and well.

Eastbourne Old Town, a smaller sister corps located at the

impressive address of 33 Royal Sussex Crescent, nestled in a picturesque area beneath the South Downs. The corps also had a busy schedule, including band, songsters, home league, Sunday school, corps cadets, open air outreach, and Cubs and Brownies.

Five weeks after Harry and Win arrived at Eastbourne Old Town, Win gave birth to a fine healthy son on 4 July 1951 at the highly-regarded Eastbourne Maternity Home where, incidentally, future UK Prime Minister Theresa May was born five years later. The overjoyed parents named their baby John, and they gave thanks to God for this precious gift.

As would be expected, settling in to a new corps with a newborn baby was no easy task. If the baby woke in the middle of the night, Harry was happy to give Win some respite and take over when John demanded attention. It was no big sacrifice – ever since the days of his early-morning paper-boy duties and late nights tucked up in bed with a book, Harry could cope with a minimum of sleep.

The comrades and friends of the Old Town Corps were delighted to welcome the new baby and John Read was dedicated to God under the flag of The Salvation Army.

Life was full and rewarding for Harry and Win, as they watched their son grow and spent their days in leadership at the corps, with its busy and varied schedule of activities, not least outreach into the community. Their pastoral spirit and innovative programs ensured that Eastbourne Old Town corps was alive and well.

A highlight for Harry was when he invited Colonel Catherine Baird, his poet mentor at the Training College, to spend a Sunday at corps. He interviewed her during the meetings and delighted in her company, although he had to confess that, as husband, father and corps officer, his days allowed little time for poetic pursuits.

During their time at Eastbourne Old Town, Harry and Win were happily looking forward to the birth of their second child. Four weeks after celebrating their second Christmas at the corps it was time for Harry to take Win to the same maternity home where John had been born, and on 23 January 1953, six days after Win's birthday, the announcement was made: "It's a boy!" Everyone was delighted – especially the two grandmothers and those at the corps – and Win and Harry were overjoyed to welcome another healthy son who they named Peter.

The matron in charge of the maternity home was a kindly Christian lady who knew and admired The Salvation Army. Win and Peter were due to return home on a Saturday morning but, knowing that Harry would be taken up with the responsibilities of leading meetings over the weekend, the matron suggested that he pick them up on the following Monday morning. It was a thoughtful gesture that had immense consequences.

Monday morning came and Harry was up early, preparing to bring Win and Peter home. There was a knock on the door at 8 am and when he opened it Harry was startled to see their doctor on the doorstep. The GP was to deliver some unbelievably heartbreaking news. During the extended time baby Peter spent in the maternity home he had contracted a virus and because his immune system was undeveloped he was dying.

Harry immediately rushed to the maternity home to be with Win, and Peter died within two or three hours. Because the baby was in isolation, Win and Harry were unable to hold him either in his last moments or afterwards.

"As with all other parents, our love had grown with Peter's anticipated birth," Harry says. "It was a love that would never be fulfilled. Our faith remained firm but it was a hard experience and, although it happened many years ago, our memories of and love for our newly-born and newly-lost child remained forever fresh in our hearts."

During this heart-wrenching time, Win and Harry were showered with love and support from family, friends and comrades of the corps. Win's mother travelled to Eastbourne to be with her after she arrived home from hospital, and it was decided that Win and John would go back to Mexborough for three weeks.

A poem Harry wrote many years later articulates the deep grief and sadness he and Win felt at that time:

Some things our hearts can hardly understand,
Stern facts that seldom can be reconciled;
We cannot think that these the Lord has planned,
Especially the passing of a child.

If God is love, how can this sadness come?
How can he let this tragedy take place?
Our hearts feel pain – our minds feel numb;
If only we could feel his healing grace!

But healing grace is closer than we know;
The Christ who bore our suffering on the cross
Has grace enough our hearts to overflow
And love enough to share with us our loss.

Although the mysteries of death remain,
Within the saddest heart Christ's peace can reign.

"One of the first things I learned at this time was just how frequent this sad experience is and how many people there are who have never been helped to carry the burden," Harry says. "The other lesson was that, following our experience, both Win and I had a quality in our ministry that could come no other way. We would, of course, have preferred not to have had that experience but the Lord has certainly used it."

Arising from his own sense of loss, it occurred to Harry that there were other families who had suffered the same kind of loss and needed guidance and help. Looking up the local newspaper, he discovered the addresses of people who had lost a child and paid them a visit. When, in Salvation Army uniform, he knocked at the door, they apologised for not having money ready to give. His gentle answer was: "I haven't come to ask for money… I too have lost a child and I have come to tell you that I am praying for you. Is there anything else I can do for you?" Harry's caring response to such a personal tragedy led to the development of a strong ministry among others who had been bereaved of their children.

Buoyed by the grace of God and the love and care of the corps community, Harry and Win continued their work at the corps, their abiding faith an inspiration to all those who knew and loved them. A few months later came the news that they had received farewell orders to Portslade, just 30 miles west of Eastbourne.

After such an eventful time at Eastbourne Old Town, farewelling their comrades was difficult not only for Harry and Win but also for the corps community, and emotions were high at their final meeting. A few days later, Harry, Win and John, by this time nearly two years old, set off for Portslade, another corps with an interesting history.

The Salvation Army started operations in Portslade in 1882, with meetings held above a shop in a building later converted into the Picturedrome Cinema. In 1910 a new citadel was opened on the corner of Church Street and North Road, and the Portslade Corps flourished.

During the Great Depression of the 1930s, however, a large number of people from the corps either emigrated or moved to other parts of England in search of employment. When Harry researched the statistics he found that one week there was an attendance of 150 and very soon afterwards it was less than half that, an exodus from which the corps had never recovered.

"In our new situation it was borne in on me that the best way of growing a corps was through faith," Harry says. "True, we had to work hard but faith was the key."

It was customary at that time in the UK for every corps and centre to have a campaign during the first week in November, with plans required to be submitted to Divisional Headquarters. For instance, campaign meetings would be held on band practice and songster practice nights, to which all were welcome, and Sunday meetings would have a focus on soul-saving.

Harry and Win decided to designate the outreach as a faith campaign, with comrades asked to especially pray for family and friends. The climax of the week at the Sunday evening meeting would be a powerful play written by Commissioner Alfred Gilliard and performed by comrades of the corps.

In a further spirit of faith and prayer, at the outset it would be announced at the corps that a Sunday meeting would be held on a pre-announced date in January to enrol converts from the campaign, with the specific aim of welcoming six new soldiers. Some of the comrades gasped when Harry launched this plan at a census board meeting, as did those who attended a special soldiers' meeting, but there was a positive response.

During the campaign there were a number of seekers including family and friends of corps members, especially of those taking part in the drama. On the enrolment night in January, Senior-Captain Bill Burrows from the International Headquarters Editorial Department, who had been invited to lead this special meeting, enrolled five brand-new soldiers and re-accepted a comrade back into the fellowship.

Hearing about the good news at Portslade, Lieut-Commissioner Frederick Coutts, the training commissioner, invited Harry to a Training College spiritual day to speak to the cadets about the faith campaign and how it had revitalised The Salvation Army's witness in Portslade.

As for members of the corps, encouraged by Harry and Win and enlivened by this answer to prayer, they increased their evangelistic efforts, taking part in pub raids and visiting former comrades and friends, inviting them to the Sunday meetings. In the vibrant spirit of faith generated at Portslade, 36 new soldiers were enrolled in 18 months and the meetings resounded with prayers of praise and thanks to God.

As Christmas 1954 approached, Harry and Win were at the Portslade Citadel with some of the comrades, busily setting up stalls for a forthcoming sale of work to raise funds for the corps. When Harry returned to the nearby quarters to pick up something that was needed, he was surprised to find a hand-delivered letter bearing a Salvation Army crest. On reading it, he hurried back to the citadel to quietly break the news to Win – they had been appointed to the Training College as from 31 December, just three weeks away!

Those few weeks passed in a flurry of busyness as Harry and Win prepared not only for Christmas celebrations but also their farewell meeting at the corps, while at the same time packing their bags for their imminent departure to the Training College.

7

WORDS AND MUSIC

We're going to sing the gospel story,
We're going to turn the world upside down.

~ HARRY READ

There was an inescapable sense of déjà vu for Captain Harry Read as he reported for duty at the International Training College early in the New Year of 1955, six and a half years after heading out as a young lieutenant to his first field appointment at Dorking.

The reason for the short notice given prior to his move was because Major Gordon Cox, the field training officer, who inspired the cadets with his warm personality and unique way with words, was unexpectedly (in Salvation Army terms) promoted to Glory. He had led the usual cadets Thursday night meeting at Camberwell and passed away overnight. He was sadly missed.

Major Cox's passing necessitated a reorganisation of the men's side of the Training College, with one of the sectional officers being promoted to field training officer and Harry appointed to take his place. As a sectional officer, Harry had 50 cadets and three cadet sergeants under his care, being responsible for their overall welfare and spiritual development, including the study of the Bible and Salvation Army doctrine, and overseeing evangelical outreaches.

There were 211 cadets in the 1954-55 Soul Winners session, including those from overseas, and the training principal, Lieut-Commissioner Frederick Coutts, warmly welcomed Harry as a sectional officer. It was a significant year for the college, being the 75th anniversary of the commencement of the training of officers, and the 25th anniversary of the opening of the William Booth Memorial Training College at Denmark Hill.

One of the cadets under Harry's supervision as a sectional officer was John Gowans, a future world leader of The Salvation Army, who had farewelled from Harry's home corps of Grangetown. "I had much to do with John," Harry says. "He was a great communicator with a lively sense of humour and was highly regarded by his fellow cadets. When he was commissioned as a cadet sergeant he proved his excellence."

With memories of their time at Portslade still fresh in their minds, and looking ahead to the future, Harry, Win and 3½-year-old John settled in to their new quarters, situated not far from the Training College.

When Harry received his appointment as a sectional officer, Win was clearly told there was no role for her, even though she had been a brilliant teacher. "Over the years we have erred in our evaluation of women," Harry says. "Women are, generally speaking, more spiritually aware than men and most churches, including The Salvation Army, have more women members than men. William and Catherine Booth had it right."

And history bears him out. Long before suffragettes were fighting for women's rights in the early 20th century, proactive Salvation Army women were already a familiar sight on English city streets by day and night, braving backstreet opium dens and tending to drunkards and the homeless. Little wonder William Booth was moved to declare, "Some of my best men are women!" His wife and Army co-founder Catherine Booth, who once confessed to being at more at home on the platform than in the kitchen, was undoubtedly one of Booth's 'best men'.

Win was to find her own way. She became the assistant home league secretary at nearby Catford Corps and soon blessed and endeared herself to the women of the corps. She was also adept at one-on-one evangelism and had a lovely way, Harry says, of getting right into the hearts and families of those she met. "Win was a wonderful role model, and such a natural talker about Jesus in a healthy and beautiful way, to the unconverted as well as with the converted."

On first encountering ladies in the neighbourhood she would introduce herself and tell them she was a Salvation Army officer, which usually led to a conversation that interested her listeners. Win started a women's group that initially met in the quarters and then expanded to such an extent that it was held in a room at the local school.

In the meantime, Harry was immersed in his work at the Training College. Travelling by train to Denmark Hill, he was invariably seated at his desk early in the morning. During the course of the day he led classes as well as conferring with other leaders to discuss programs, and in the evening he had meetings and interviews with cadets, usually arriving home at 8.30 or 9 pm.

The designated Friday afternoon off allowed for some breathing space, but weekends were spoken for. Saturdays and Sundays were spent with cadets at a training corps, with open air meetings, pub raids and evening meetings on both days. All venues had to be reached by public transport, which could be time-consuming and sometimes unreliable. Transport times improved for Harry when, after a few years at the Training College, he acquired a moped – a motorised bicycle that could also be pedalled.

Five months after Harry arrived at the college, the commissioning of the 216 Soul Winners sergeants and cadets was held on 13 May at the Royal Albert Hall, with Harry farewelling the cadets and cadet sergeants of his group. Preparations then had to be made to welcome the Sword Bearers, a session of 175 cadets, that was due to begin in August.

By August that year, however, Harry had more pressing things on his mind. Since arriving at the college, he and Win had been happily looking forward to the birth of their third child and in early August the time came for Win to be admitted to the Mothers' Hospital, a maternity hospital in Lower Clapton Road, Hackney. Initially established by The Salvation Army in 1912 to serve women of London's East End, the hospital was taken over by the National Health Service in 1948, but continued to operate with Salvation Army midwives until 1986.

As it was the norm for expectant mothers to be admitted to hospital a few days before the baby's birth, during that time Harry answered his phone at the Training College with an involuntary intake of breath, anticipating a call from the hospital with the good news. And good news it was! On 4 August 1955, Win and Harry became the delighted parents of a beautiful baby girl, Margaret, a little sister for John.

Harry immediately jumped on his pushbike and pedalled the seven miles from the Training College to the hospital via the Blackwall Tunnel, the only major road crossing the Thames in East London, including several sharp bends along the way. "Getting to the level portion of the tunnel is quite easy," Harry says, "but then there is a long pull on the way out and, as at the time there was no overtaking allowed, you can imagine how blessed I was by motorists coming up behind me. When I got to the Mothers' Hospital, from the moment I saw and held Margaret she became my favourite daughter and has remained so ever since."

God keeps reminding us that he is love,
That love defines him, in him reigns supreme.
And when a child is born it seems to prove
Love is reality – not just a dream.

From his own tenderness a child is given,
A sign of love, a promise wisely made,
Enabling earth to have a taste of heaven,
For where love is, heaven's love is being displayed.

We look upon this infant and we know
There are no limits to her present worth,
Unlimited her future as she grows,
Such is her great potential from her birth.

Like every child this infant is unique,
Distinctive in her personality
But in our prayers for her just now, we seek
God and his love as her security.

It was a measure of many Salvation Army officers' dedication and sacrifice that some like Harry, with such a time-consuming workload, saw little of their families. Leaving for the college early in the morning while John and Margaret were still tucked up in bed and returning home late in the evening when they were again back in bed – not to mention weekends away with the cadets – meant that time Harry spent with Win and the children was at a premium.

August was a busy month, as it also saw the intake of the 1955-56 Sword Bearers session at the Training College. And so the residential period from August to May began again, with Harry as sectional officer supervising the intensive study and activities of lectures, Bible classes and practical field training for the cadets, as well as the workload of the cadet sergeants for whom he was responsible.

Following the commissioning of the Sword Bearers, the next intake of cadets at the Training College was named the Faithful session, and included young men and women not only from the British Isles but also from India, Japan, the West Indies and several European countries.

One of the cadets in Harry's section was a young man by the name of John Larsson, an 18-year-old Swedish Salvationist who had led a cosmopolitan life from childhood while living with his officer parents in their appointments in Denmark, Chile and Argentina. Kindred spirits from their first meeting, the lives of Harry and John were to become intertwined throughout their service as Salvation Army officers.

Cadet John Larsson, who 44 years later was to become The Salvation Army's 17th General, declared in his autobiography, *Saying Yes to Life*, that no other officer had been more influential in his life than Harry Read, describing him as his "father-in-God and role model". During their time at the Training College over the next few years, Harry and his protégé were to become partners in a memorable songwriting collaboration.

The following year when the 1957-58 Courageous session was welcomed to the Training College, a change in leadership had taken place. The training principal, Lieut-Commissioner Frederick Coutts, had been promoted to the rank of commissioner and appointed as the territorial commander of the Australia Eastern Territory. His successor was Lieut-Commissioner Kaare Westergaard, a Danish officer, who inspired the cadets with his enthusiasm and lively personality.

When the cadets in Harry's section participated in weekend campaigns at various corps in the London area, it was usual on a Saturday night for a short play written by Commissioner Alfred Gilliard to be presented. After one such performance, because he'd seen it so many times, a bandsman with a cheeky grin on his face said to Harry, "If a cadet is ill, just let me know and I can fill that part for you."

"So we chuckled over it," Harry says, "but I wasn't chuckling inside. The more I thought about it the more I was thinking that we should do something different. Then the Lord seemed to be saying to me, 'You must start writing, Harry.'"

That experience was the catalyst for Harry to head to his typewriter and write a succession of dramatic presentations to specifically speak to the hearts and minds of those in the corps the cadets visited.

After he got "the bit between his teeth", Harry says, he realised the potential for such performances to also be held in open air meetings and on the steps of the local town hall. When this happened, especially if the participants wore costumes, the presentations drew large crowds.

Harry was also asked to help produce the Friday evening pageants that were held as the climax of the two meetings in the Royal Albert Hall on the day of commissioning. The hour-long pageants involved the cadets in a large-scale dramatic presentation, with music by the singing brigade and cadets' band a prominent part of the proceedings. Harry admits that up until then he thought those pageants were rather predictable.

During Harry's time at the Training College, Win continued her work at the Catford Corps, with her unobtrusive caring ministry endearing her to everyone she met. Harry remembers that John had made friends with Stephen, a boy who lived across the road from their quarters, and he often spent time there. In a terrible accident, the boy's father, a plumber, was working in the loft when an electrical problem resulted in him being killed instantly.

When Win heard about this she immediately visited the boy's distraught mother who said through her tears, "I knew you would come, Win."

In 1960 a marked change was taking place at the Training College, with a newly-instigated two-year training programme for cadets. The Soldiers of Christ session were the first to experience training where the first year concentrated on the theoretical, including study of the scriptures and Salvation Army doctrine, history, principles and procedures. The next year was then devoted to the experiential and practical, with the summer period and much of the second year spent in corps, social and goodwill appointments.

"When the cadets came to the college they wanted few things more than trying to save the world," Harry says. "True, they knew study was important but they were soul-winners first and foremost, hoping and expecting to find fulfilment there. Members of staff, including me, were voluble about the need to get our priorities right. It didn't take long to create the right kind of programme." Eventually the training schedule was modified to give equal emphasis to the academic and practical and intersperse them throughout the two years.

It was also in 1960 that Harry received a letter from the training principal, Commissioner Westergaard, asking him to write the commissioning pageant for the 200 cadets of the Greathearts session. Exhilarated by the request, Harry thought he should discuss his plans with Colonel Hubert Goddard, the chief side officer, telling him he wanted to change the traditional format and do something quite different. "That's the reason you've been asked to write the pageant," was the reassuring answer.

What Harry had in mind was a full-scale musical production, and as he wrote the script and lyrics for the songs he thought about who could best write the music. One name immediately came to mind. With his undoubted musical ability, who better than Lieutenant John Larsson, Harry said to himself.

After being appointed as a cadet sergeant in Harry's section, and serving for one year as the corps officer of the Sunderland Southwick and Washington Corps, John Larsson had been reappointed to the Training College as a house officer, once again under Harry's supervision.

Harry showed the script to John and asked how he would feel about writing the music for the songs. "I'd love to!" was the answer. So began a words and music partnership that saw the successful production of commissioning pageants for the next three years, with the last, 'God's Soldier', written for the Soldiers of Christ session in 1962, being the culmination of the combined Read-Larsson sanctified skills.

Harry also enlisted the support of Lieutenant Joy Webb, the leader of the women cadets' singing brigade, telling her he had in mind that, rather than being static during the pageant, the singers would move around the stage as they sang. He was delighted with her cooperation and support.

The Musician reported on the performance of 'God's Soldier' at the Soldiers of Christ commissioning pageant, as "an exciting view of new possibilities in the use of Army music in making known the Army's message and mission".

One of the scenes in the pageant depicted an open air meeting and, in an electrifying moment, the play-acting suddenly became reality when the leader made his appeal and a number of seekers rose from the audience and knelt on-stage in the open air ring.

"The giant, joyous, swaying chorus became a vast earnest praying chorus, softly singing as the penitents made their way forward. Cadets disguised as 'coffee bar types' forgot their role in the pageant while they knelt to pray with the seekers," the *Musician* report said.

The song 'God's Soldier Marches as to War', written for this memorable pageant, was to become an often-sung and well-loved anthem of The Salvation Army.

God's soldier marches as to war,
A soldier on an alien shore,
A soldier true, a soldier who
Will keep the highest aims in view.
God's soldier goes where sin is found;
Where evil reigns, his battleground;
A cunning foe to overthrow
And strike for truth a telling blow.

Chorus:
We're going to fill, fill, fill the world with glory;
We're going to smile, smile, smile and not frown;
We're going to sing, sing, sing the gospel story;
We're going to turn the world upside down.

God's soldier has to stand alone,
Accepting burdens not his own;
A lonely work he cannot shirk,
Where dark and deadly dangers lurk.
God's soldier must courageous be,
And from his duties never flee,
For millions wait whose need is great,
And he must not God's plan forsake.

Harry recounts the sometimes complicated trajectory of collaborative songwriting, at the same time admitting that his non-musical brain presents him with problems. If the music is written first, he asks the composer to record the tune with one finger because he finds chords a distraction. He then plays the tune over and over again until he has sorted out the metre and the mood, adding that 'words first' is his preference.

"'God's Soldier' is not a bad example of co-operation," Harry says. "In the first place I wrote four verses of four lines each and gave John Larsson a small selection of possible choruses. The verses were intended to be fairly serious and the chorus an explosion of joy. The more John worked at it the more he drew a blank until one day he asked if I could develop one of the potential choruses a little more, and this I did. After some time, John told me he could do it better if the four four-line verses could become two eight-line verses, so the four verses became two."

When, unbeknown to Harry, the song was accepted by the International Music Board, he offered to write a third verse but the board was more than happy with two. John Larsson had written a stirring coda but when the song was published it had been omitted. When Harry and John commented about the omission, Colonel Charles Skinner, head of the Music Editorial Department, included the coda in his 'Songs of the Soldier' band selection.

The triumphant and memorable commissioning celebrations for the Soldiers of Christ session were a fitting conclusion to the seven and a half years Harry spent as a sectional officer at the International Training College, with hundreds of cadets benefiting from his spirituality, care and encouragement. It was a time he describes – with the exception of the lack of family time – as "for a youngish man, the best appointment imaginable".

With Harry and Win's pastoral hearts always at the centre of their service, they were delighted to receive news of their forthcoming appointment as corps officers of the Hanwell Corps, eight miles west of the City of London.

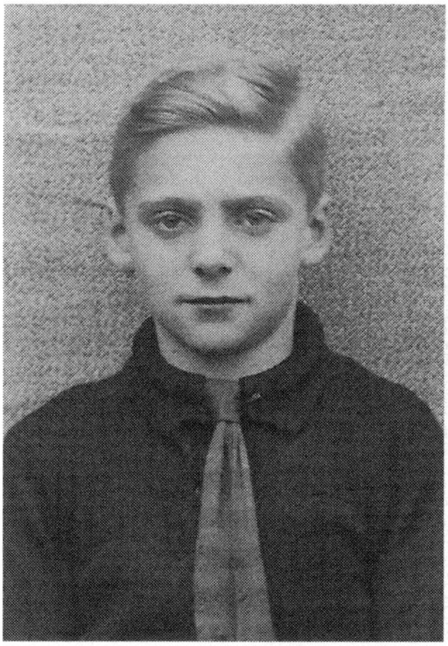

God gives his children hope —
A hope for better things,
An urge for life of wider scope
Than mere existence brings.
Instinctively we feel
That we have but to reach
And God new ventures will reveal,
New truths our hearts will teach.

~ HARRY READ

CLARAMARA
SCAWFELL

ROYAL CORPS OF SIGNALS

Cadet Harry Read

On the campaign trail

Harry commissioned at Royal Albert Hall

Lieutenants Harry Read and Ted Cotterill, Dorking corps officers

Above: Newlyweds Harry and Win

Left: Corps officers at Chichester

Below: Love is in the air

Top left: Win, Harry and baby John

Top right: Harry and Margaret at the seaside

Centre left: Another family beach day

Centre right: Win, Margaret (with her teddy bear) and John

Right: Family meal time

With the home league ladies at Chichester

Self Denial weekend with the help of cadets

Scotland Territorial Summer Music School
at Middleton Camp, Gorebridge, Midlothian near Edinburgh

John and Anne married on 17 July 1976

God's fingerprints are on your wedding day
A day which came to you gift-wrapped with love,
More than your hearts can feel, or words can say,
This love your life's experience will prove.

~ HARRY READ

Margaret and Graham married on 11 June 1977

8

LEADING WITH LOVE

Set an example for the believers in speech, in conduct,
in love, in faith and in purity.
~ TITUS 2:7

The official date of the appointment of Captain and Mrs Harry Read to Hanwell Corps, a thriving Salvation Army centre in a pleasant West London suburb, was Thursday 17 May 1962, coincidentally Harry's 38th birthday.

The following Sunday, Harry, Win and their two children, John, 11, and Margaret, 6, were given a rousing welcome by comrades and friends of the Hanwell Corps, which had been at work in the area for 71 years. The Salvation Army registered a lecture hall for worship there in 1891 and moved to a building in Station Road in 1903. In 1905 they acquired the former Wesleyan Chapel in Lower Boston Road and 57 years later the corps was alive and well.

"There was a plethora of very good Salvation Army corps in the long stretch from the West End of London right down to Heathrow and beyond, with a strong Army presence in the area," Harry says. "Ealing and Hanwell Corps were very close, with no more than a mile and a half between the two."

When Harry and Win arrived, activities at Hanwell Corps were in full swing, including a large band and songster brigade, with an active evangelical programme including three open airs on Sundays. Some years earlier the corps acquired an adjacent building which became the youth centre, and work with young people, including Sunday school, youth group and corps cadets, was flourishing, as was the home league.

Mindful of the many demands on Harry's time, Win suggested

she take responsibility for the young people's work and the home league, liaising with the young people's sergeant major and the home league secretary. Harry was more than happy to agree.

"Win was remarkably gifted in so many ways." Harry says. "She could lead people with great ease, and they followed her with pleasure because she was so sweetly reasonable. She was also a great visitor and if anyone new came to the corps Win would be on their doorstep in a flash, welcoming them into the corps fellowship. Because of her influence, mothers of Sunday school children came to the home league, and children and grandchildren of home leaguers also attended the corps. This was Win at her very best."

An added blessing to Harry and Win's move to Hanwell was being able to spend more time together as a family now that Harry's daily commute and long hours at the Training College were no more. He especially treasured the realisation by Margaret that she now had a dad who was there when she woke up in the morning and who could often tuck her into bed at night. From her earliest days when Harry was at the Training College Margaret saw very little of him and, although the bonding had always been there, at Hanwell their father-daughter relationship blossomed into a lovely affinity that they still enjoy today.

Harry also enjoyed spending time with John, who was then of high school age. Especially pleasing was the opportunity for him to be accepted into a highly-regarded grammar school, St Clement Danes, in Hammersmith because he had done so well in the 11-plus exam that governs admission to schools using academic achievement as a criterion for scholarships. St Clement Danes was eight miles from Hanwell and John caught a bus and a train to and from school during the week. Margaret went to the local state school and enjoyed her time there.

In the meantime, Harry and Win were in their element as they immersed themselves in leadership of the corps, their pastoral hearts being the hallmark of their officership. They were ably assisted at Hanwell by a full complement of local officers. The corps was also financially self-sufficient, as the comrades and friends were fully committed in their stewardship and, in Salvation Army terms, faithfully 'fired their cartridge' of tithes and offerings each week.

The music sections were a shining example of Salvation Army commitment and participation at its best. Some years earlier Reg Ketteringham, a talented musician, his wife Moira and their three sons, Ken, Kelvin and Keith, transferred from a country corps to Hanwell. Reg had a special gift for training youngsters in brass banding and very soon Hanwell had an excellent young people's band. He also visited the parents of the young people, winning their support, and many of the parents started attending the corps. The keen young bandsmen eventually became the heart of the senior band which, by the time Harry and Win arrived at the corps, numbered more than 30 players, with an average age of 23. Reg's son Ken eventually became the senior bandmaster.

The songster brigade, under their leader Sam Hooper, was also a talented and dedicated musical section of the corps. Harry says that Sam was an outstanding songster leader, reckoning he could have even made the dummies in Madame Tussauds sing! Sam had high expectations, requiring the songsters to sing from memory, adding to the stirring impact of their witness. To this day 78 RPM Regal Zonophone recordings of Hanwell Songsters singing well-known hymns including 'The Saviour's Name', 'Jesus, Keep Me Near the Cross' and 'The Old Rugged Cross' are being offered online.

The band and songsters were often mentioned in The Salvation Army's *Musician* magazine and because of their excellence were in great demand to visit other corps, which both sections would undertake four times a year. Because either the band or the songsters were away on different occasions for a total of eight weeks a year, Harry felt that such frequent absences meant they could hardly run the best programme at the corps. He spoke to Bandmaster Ketteringham and Songster Leader Hooper and to their great credit they agreed to reduce the number of visits to other corps.

One of Sam Hooper's closest friends at the corps was Eric Ball, described as "one of the most prolific writers and influential figures in the brass band and choral world", who was eventually honoured with an Order of the British Empire. A former Salvation Army officer with a superb record of musical leadership, Eric and his wife Olive had attended the Hanwell Corps for a number of years.

Visiting Eric and Olive at home was always a pleasure, Harry says. Whenever he called on them, Olive would warmly invite him in, knock on the door of Eric's study and say, "The captain's here." Eric would appear and join Harry and Olive for a lively conversation, followed by a Bible reading and prayer.

Harry couldn't help feeling a little guilty at such visits. Some years earlier, he'd read about English poet Samuel Taylor Coleridge, who had been writing a poem after experiencing a vision of Paradise in a dream. Coleridge had written the first 54 lines when a knock at the door heralded a visitor, who he greeted warmly. When the visitor left and Coleridge returned to his work he couldn't – and never did – recover the inspiration that had been broken by the visitor. The lines were of such quality that they were published under the title of 'Kubla Khan' but the full masterpiece had been lost because of the unintentional intrusion of the visitor.

Harry often wondered if he was the same sort of distraction to Eric that Coleridge's visitor had been, adding that he was always made more than welcome. He need not have worried. In 1962, during Harry's time at Hanwell, Eric Ball composed one of his most celebrated works, the magnificent tone poem 'The Kingdom Triumphant'. This epic composition was published in the Festival Series Brass Band Journal in July 1963 and became a classic of brass band repertoire, being performed by five Salvation Army bands and a 1000-voice chorus, conducted by Eric Ball himself, at the Army's 1978 International Congress.

While he was at Hanwell, Harry received a phone call from Colonel Ivy Mawby, a friend of his from early Training College days, now the national home league secretary. Ivy asked if he would write and produce an entertaining item for the upcoming national home league rally to be held in the Methodist Central Hall.

In those days there was an advertising campaign with the slogan

'Behind every successful man there's a woman'. Harry reversed that to 'Behind every successful woman there's a man' and wrote a humorous 15-minute sketch. Because the sketch involved a lot of men, he enlisted the 30-plus Hanwell bandsmen to become involved. He also needed a pianist to carry it through and Win suggested Eric Ball, who was very receptive when Harry asked him.

"To see the face of Eric looking out over the top of the piano, getting all his cues right, and our band doing the dialogue, choreography and singing, with convulsions of laughter ringing around the hall, was a sight to behold," Harry says.

Afterwards Eric told Harry how much he enjoyed taking part, going on to recount that during World War II he belonged to an official War Office entertainment group, ENSA, the Entertainments National Service Association, that travelled all over the country entertaining servicemen and women. As the pianist, Eric accompanied dancers and singers – exotic and otherwise – as well as serious vocal soloists. "No wonder he took our burlesque in his stride," Harry says with a smile.

Another priority for the corps was the annual Self Denial Appeal, begun in 1886 after General William Booth delivered a stirring challenge in London's Exeter Hall, calling on Salvationists to deny themselves and give sacrificially to support The Salvation Army's work in countries devastated by poverty and natural disasters. As well as Salvationists personally practising self-denial, additional funds were raised by door-knocking in the community.

The area allocated to the Hanwell Corps was relatively small due to the number of other corps in surrounding districts but collecting was reliant each year on the same small group of Salvationists. In an effort to share the load Harry enlisted the help of a large number of corps members, allocating to each one a fundraising target and a certain number of houses to visit in a specific area. This innovation was such a success that in a short time the target set by Divisional Headquarters was considerably exceeded.

Knowing there was a nearby corps where, largely because of health problems, they were struggling to maintain the level of collecting needed in order to reach their target, Harry spoke to the Hanwell local officers and the divisional commander, gaining their agreement before sending a substantial sum of Hanwell's Self Denial funds to the other corps.

"This blessed them immensely," Harry says, "and I've had friends for life from the family of the corps officers we helped. Some years ago I was invited to be a guest speaker at a commemoration service in Hyde Park run by the Royal Society of St George. Afterwards a chap came over and introduced himself as the son of the officers we helped in those Hanwell days. He is a very active Christian and a substantial businessman and, all these years later, still keeps in touch with me."

Pub booming was another of the outreaches in Hanwell, and although the corps did not have a large district there were quite a number of pubs in the area, including as far as Brentford. On Friday and Saturday nights Harry and two or three others from the corps were a regular presence at the local hotels. One man, a builder, who had been contacted in the pubs, joined the corps with his wife, and subsequently carried out lots of useful jobs at the hall and quarters.

Another activity at Hanwell Corps was the out-training of cadets from the Training College, which was in reasonable proximity to the corps. Knowing from his time at the college that sometimes cadets were largely left to their own devices when visiting corps, ever the innovator Harry devised a plan that concentrated on far more proactive training and, after consultation with the field training officer, wasted no time in putting that plan into action.

Typically, a Training College group consisted of 12 cadets and a sergeant and, as well as taking part in meetings and open air activities on Sundays at Hanwell, they were given hands-on experience in the whole gamut of corps activities throughout the week. Training in young people's work included organising special meetings for the children and visitation of their parents; the cadets visited the home league and the newly-formed over 60s club; and they participated in pub booming and door-to-door visitation, noting the names and addresses of the people so that a follow-up contact could be arranged for those who showed interest.

The Hanwell local officers were also involved in advising the cadets, including the corps sergeant major and the treasurer of the corps, a retired officer who put them through their paces regarding the handling of corps finances.

The cadets' training programme became very much a part of the corps activities, with their visits of six weeks' duration being followed by another group of cadets soon afterwards. Rather than hindering the corps programme, the cadets became co-workers with Harry, Win and the comrades, and their presence brought an added vibrancy to the gatherings. "Things were buzzing in the corps and everyone was very positive," Harry says.

With memories of Harry's time at the Training College still fresh in his mind, it was with a great deal of pleasure that two young people were farewelled to the Training College from Hanwell during Harry and Win's time there.

A few years earlier, a young man named Gilbert Ellis, who also went to the Training College from Hanwell Corps, was one of the cadets under Harry's care as sectional officer. Gilbert married Reidun, a Norwegian officer, and served as an executive officer in Norway, travelling extensively in his work for God and the Army. The joke between Gilbert and Harry was that the first thing Harry did for him after being appointed to the Hanwell Corps was to remove Gilbert – who was now in charge of a Salvation Army corps in another location – from the roll, an action usually reserved for non-attenders and miscreants.

While Harry and Win were happy and fulfilled in their leadership at Hanwell, personal finances were tight and, as they were unable to afford a car, Harry was still relying on his moped to putter around the neighbourhood. For the first time in their corps officership there was a telephone provided in the quarters and, as for television, the family watched news and programmes on the small set they had bought a few years earlier while at the Training College.

"Not many of us could afford to buy or rent a TV set at first," Harry says, "but both International Headquarters and National Headquarters were fully aware of its importance. With our social work, music and compelling leadership, including General Albert Orsborn, members of the Founder's household including Commissioner Catherine Bramwell-Booth, and other evangelists, The Salvation Army had much to offer."

On Thursday 1 October 1963, a significant date in Salvation Army history, Harry was delighted to hear the news that, following the retirement of General Wilfred Kitching, Commissioner Frederick Coutts, Harry's friend and mentor, had been elected as the 8th General of The Salvation Army, to take office as from 23 November.

News outlets were quick to interview the new worldwide leader of The Salvation Army and at the first press conference following his election General Coutts made what could be considered a rather off-the-cuff remark that it would certainly be possible to take the gospel message to coffee bars with electric guitars if these proved to be an effective method.

Ever alert to ground-breaking news, the media was keen to report on this innovation, and a rather hastily convened pop group was formed at the Training College, with Captain Joy Webb, who was eventually to receive the Order of the Founder, taking charge. Members were from the current Proclaimers of the Faith session, including Bill Davidson, Peter Dalziel, Sylvia Gair and Wycliffe Noble. Under the leadership of Joy Webb, they were to be known as the Joystrings and within months their single 'It's an Open Secret' was No. 32 on the music charts.

Harry was delighted at the news, commenting that the advent of the Joystrings, which at the time sparked more than a little controversy, made a huge difference at the Training College and subsequently to the media presence of The Salvation Army in the United Kingdom. He was also pleased that Joy Webb, who he had worked closely with on the commissioning pageants, was instrumental in forming the group.

After two fulfilling and rewarding years at Hanwell Corps, Harry and Win received farewell orders during a personal interview with British Commissioner Edgar Grinsted. It was with mixed feelings that they farewelled; Hanwell was a corps that would always be close to their hearts. It was their first corps back on the Salvation Army field after seven years at the Training College and the last corps they were to command, as their subsequent appointments were in executive positions.

"We were not overjoyed at leaving," Harry says, "because we were having such a blessed and refreshing time there. We were building the corps, new people were coming in, the young people's work was growing and the home league was thriving. We had a marvellous time and they were great days.

"Win and I always viewed ourselves as corps officers," Harry adds, "and, though we were to spend many years in other appointments, we never lost that conviction. Always, at heart, we were corps officers."

9

LADS AND LASSIES

The flower of youth never appears more beautiful than when it bends towards the sun of righteousness.

~ MATTHEW HENRY

After a memorable farewell from the comrades and friends of the Hanwell Corps, Harry, Win, John and Margaret travelled to Paisley in Scotland, where the newly-promoted Major Harry Read had been appointed as divisional youth secretary of the South West Scotland Division as from 14 May 1964.

And the times they were a'changing. The so-called Swinging Sixties was a decade of largely youth-driven social and cultural change, with the first teenage generation since World War II free from conscription in Britain. Beatlemania, psychedelic art, hippies and mini-skirts were regularly reported on by the media, as well as the introduction of transistor radios, microwave ovens, credit cards, cassette tapes, supermarkets and colour television, not to mention the contraceptive pill and the women's liberation movement.

This changing worldview would also have an impact on Harry's leadership of The Salvation Army's children's and youth ministries in the division, as to resonate with this age group it was important to understand their mindset and attitudes. By now John was a teenager and Margaret was nine years old, and their perspective was invaluable in Harry's leadership while keeping abreast of the times.

Harry, Win and the family soon settled in to their new home in Paisley, a large town and industrial centre seven miles west of Glasgow, once famous for its weaving and textile industries. John and Margaret, with the admirable resilience shown in children of officers who were frequently moved to new appointments, quickly adapted to their new schools.

After being given farewell orders from Hanwell, Harry visited John's headmaster at St Clement Danes school, enquiring about suitable schools in the Paisley area. Without hesitation he recommended Paisley Grammar School, promising to write to the headmaster there. Soon after their arrival, Harry requested an interview with the head of the school, who warmly welcomed him and said, "We'll have to give John a test but I'm feeling in my heart that a Dean of the Scottish Church will be able to help The Salvation Army." After passing the test with flying colours, John became a student at Paisley Grammar.

Margaret was enrolled at the local primary school, situated in the next street to where they lived. After being teased by her Scottish classmates about her English accent, Margaret – being a quick learner, Harry says – very soon spoke perfect 'Paisley', complete with Scottish burr, while John resolutely retained his accustomed South London accent.

Harry and Win were welcomed to the South West Scotland Division by the divisional commander, Brigadier Thomas Goodwin. As divisional youth secretary, Harry was responsible for the development, planning and implementation of various children's and young people's programmes, as well as liaising with the corps officers in the approximately 30 corps of the division.

"It was certainly a very interesting and rewarding time," Harry says, "because I discovered that I had been the sectional officer at the Training College for many of the officers in the division. We had great rapport and a warm, creative relationship from the start."

During this time Scotland was a stand-alone Salvation Army territory, with the territorial commander responsible to the British Commissioner. The Scottish Territorial Headquarters were situated in Glasgow, under the leadership of Commissioner Albert Mingay. The territorial youth secretary was Major Ted Grainger, who was a cadet when Harry was a cadet sergeant at the Training College.

As Glasgow was only a 10-minute train trip from Paisley,

Harry and Win often went there for territorial events including young people's activities such as youth councils and music camps. Glasgow was close to Harry's heart, as it was there at a Salvation Army meeting he attended as a young paratrooper returned from the Normandy battlefields of World War II that he was called by God to be an officer in The Salvation Army.

On weekdays Harry travelled by moped to and from the divisional office in Paisley, where his colleagues included the divisional commander, general secretary, divisional secretary, finance secretary and director of women's ministries, all of whom gave him a very warm welcome. One of the lighter moments Harry recalls was during a staff conference with the divisional commander when a young employee, "fresh from school and bright as a button", knocked on the door to announce in her delightful Scottish brogue, "I've got that old geezer on the phone," that old geezer being a senior Salvation Army officer.

With specific responsibility for training each of the male cadets in children's and youth ministries during his second year at the Training College, Harry was more than qualified to mentor the corps officers in the division about ministering to children and young people. "Our work in the Training College was very positive and creative," Harry says, "directly related to the task of ministering to youngsters, and then of course when we went to Hanwell Corps we again had the opportunity of putting into action all kinds of ideas, including those for young people."

As for Win, despite her impressive credentials as a graduate teacher and years of experience in working with children, once again she had no official appointment. In the past the wife of the divisional youth secretary had taken over the supervision of The Salvation Army's Life-saving Guards and Sunbeams brigades (which had become Guides and Brownies) and this Win was happy to do, in addition to assisting Harry wherever possible in his work with children and young people.

Corps ministries in the South West Scotland Division covered children from babies to teens, including cradle roll, primary,

Sunday school, junior soldiers, singing company, junior band, corps cadets and life-saving sections, as well as prospective candidates for the Training College.

The encouragement of young people to become candidates for officership was one of Harry's priorities, having served as a sectional officer for hundreds of cadets at the Training College during his seven-year appointment there. "When I contacted officers in the division," Harry says, "I always gave a very special emphasis to candidateship." Among the many young people Harry personally spoke to about their calling was a lad named Ian Barr, who made a decision to become a junior candidate at the age of 14. Ian entered the Training College in 1973, and today is a retired lieut-colonel, an esteemed Salvation Army officer, scholar and author.

Another priority for Harry and Win was to ensure that each corps was well supplied with written material to enhance the children's ministries. *International Company Orders*, the official teaching manual for Sunday school teachers, otherwise known as company guards, had been painstakingly prepared over a number of years by Adjutant Frederick Coutts of the International Headquarters Literary Department. He had also prepared lessons for corps cadets, young people from the age of 12 who, under the guidance of a corps cadet guardian, studied the Bible, Christian doctrine and the principles and practices of The Salvation Army.

The Sunday school lessons were also included in *The Young Soldier* magazine, a big hit with young children, with a print run at that time of a quarter of a million copies. Older young people were keen readers of *The Vanguard*, a successor to *The Warrior*, which had been edited by Harry's mentor Colonel Catherine Baird.

The New Testament version of *The New English Bible* had recently been published, with the aim of the compilers to produce a Bible in "thoroughly modern English". (In 1989 it was revised and republished as the *Revised English Bible*.) "When *The New English Bible* was published, I loved it immediately," Harry says. "In fact, I memorised large chunks of it, as I once had with the Authorised Version." After conferring with Brigadier Goodwin, Harry contacted the corps officers of the division asking that junior soldiers receive a copy of *The New English Bible* Gospel when they were enrolled.

With memories of his youthful enthusiasm as a Baden Powell Cub and Scout among his happiest, Harry was delighted to regale the young people with stories of his scouting adventures whenever he visited corps to encourage life-saving activities in the division.

Win also enjoyed supervising the Army's former Guards and Sunbeams ministry. When she knew this would be part of her responsibilities she contacted the Girl Guides Association and explained what her future role was going to be. The integration of The Salvation Army's Life-Saving Scouts and Chums with the Baden Powell Scout Association and the Guards and Sunbeams with the Girl Guides Association in Britain in 1959 meant there was a warm association between the two organisations. The Girl Guides Association offered Win a full leadership training course and on completion, when she visited corps as a divisional leader, she wore the official Girl Guides uniform.

Harry's responsibilities as divisional youth secretary encompassed a wide range of activities, including public relations events, campaigns, evangelism and outreach programmes, youth camps, and discipleship of young people. "Win and I were both very much aware of the fact that our sphere of influence was there and we must use it to the glory of God," he says.

When it came to the annual divisional youth councils it was usual to hold a festival on the Saturday night beforehand featuring talented youthful participants plus massed young people's bands and singing companies of the division. As the programme drew to a close, the divisional commander would step forward and make an appeal, inviting those present to consider their faith and commitment, before the benediction was pronounced and parents waited to take their children home. "It wasn't an atmosphere that had previously produced a great deal of spiritual response," Harry says.

Recalling his experiences at the Training College where he had written a number of pageants that had a powerful impact on both the participants and the congregation, Harry saw the potential of the divisional youth councils festival to challenge and bless in a similar way.

After praying about it he formulated a plan to write a pageant to include young people from every corps in the division and, with the cooperation of the officers, to visit each corps and rehearse the parts before joining together in combined rehearsals prior the festival. Upon receiving the divisional commander's blessing, Harry set about writing a script for the pageant and contacting corps officers to seek their support. With many of them remembering taking part in the commissioning pageants at the Training College, they were enthusiastic and eager to join in.

The initial rehearsals created a sense of excitement among the youthful participants, including John and Margaret, and the combined rehearsals brought about a warm bonding between both the young people of the various corps and the officers. There was a sense of shared challenge, fellowship and interconnection.

As the crowd gathered for the youth councils festival there was much chatter and excitement. The pageant was warmly and thoughtfully received and at the conclusion a hush fell over the large congregation when the appeal was given and a number of decisions were made. It was a night that would be talked about for years to come.

Another experience that stirred Harry's memory was to follow. When he visited the Port Glasgow Corps, one of the largest corps in the division, he was welcomed by the comrades, many of whom remembered a cadets' campaign led by Harry as sectional officer a number of years before. In a conversation with the corps officer at the time, Harry discussed the difference between holy communion and a love feast. He had recently spent some time reading about love feasts, also known as agape meals, defined as a communal Christian fellowship meal where participants share in witness and praise. "Let's organise a love feast here at the corps," Harry suggested, and the corps officer was in full agreement.

Soon afterwards, a large congregation of comrades and the cadets met at the citadel, under the leadership of Harry and the corps officer, to take part in a whole new spiritual experience. Symbolic of a meal, cracker biscuits and mineral water were served and, Harry says, "It was a touching, wonderful experience. People who were fellow soldiers but not the best of friends because of something that had happened in the past began to beautifully reconcile, and the corps took enormous steps forward. Ten years later the comrades still remembered that day."

With young people's work encompassing children from birth to late teenage years, one of the delights of Harry's time as divisional youth secretary was to be asked by parents from the various corps to officiate at the dedication service of their baby. A poem he wrote many years later, especially for such joyous occasions, expresses the awe and wonder of the arrival of a newborn child:

With all love's richness and simplicity
We view this infant on this special day,
For love bespeaks its authenticity
When family and friends meet in this way.

We celebrate the love a child exudes,
The trust, the vulnerable helplessness,
The promise of God-given aptitudes,
Capacities for fun and happiness.

And in this infant, as with other bairns,
Behind, before, around stands God's great love,
And he for whom the sane world yearns
Awaits each one of us, his love to prove.

How great the gifts of life, of love, of care!
How wonderful this day is bathed in prayer!

During Harry and Win's second year at Paisley, the 1965 Centenary Celebrations were held in London from Thursday 24 June to Saturday 3 July, to mark 100 years since the founding of The Salvation Army by William and Catherine Booth. They travelled from Paisley for the celebrations as almost 2000 Salvationists from around the world converged on London, joining in fellowship with comrades from Britain. It was the largest international Salvation Army gathering ever held until that time.

The inaugural meeting at the Royal Albert Hall was graced by the presence of Queen Elizabeth II, the Archbishops of Canterbury and Westminster, and heads of state and diplomatic representatives of 40 countries who were welcomed by General Frederick Coutts. The programme featured the International Staff Band and a 500-voice centenary chorus. Harry's heart warmed within him during the afternoon when the International Staff Band played Colonel Charles Skinner's 'Songs of the Soldier', which included a rousing rendition of 'God's Soldier', the affirming, joyous song Harry had earlier written for a cadets' pageant in collaboration with Captain John Larsson.

Soon after this event the time neared for the Read family's annual furlough and Harry and Win wondered where they could go because – as always on an officer's allowance – money was tight. In a chat with the divisional commander, Harry mentioned their difficulty and Thomas Goodwin had an idea. There was a small corps in the seaside town of Prestwick that was dependent on visiting officers to lead the meetings. "Why don't you spend your furlough in the vacant quarters, lead the Sunday meetings at the corps and enjoy your two weeks there?" he said.

So Harry, Win, John and Margaret took the 40-minute train journey to Prestwick and enjoyed a two-week stay there, taking their sandwiches to the beach and soaking up the sunshine. Harry and Win also enjoyed leading the meetings and encouraging the comrades at the small local corps. Arriving home contented and relaxed, they were greeted by a neighbouring family who had splashed out on an expensive holiday to the south coast of England and came back early because of torrential rain. Chuckling at the memory, Harry says, "They were a bit miffed when they saw our suntans."

As divisional youth secretary, more often than not Harry's Sundays were spent visiting various corps, travelling either on his moped or by public transport, and enjoying warm fellowship wherever he went. Having spent some time in Stromness and Edinburgh during his military service after returning from the Normandy battlefields, Harry had a high regard for both the Scottish people and their way of life.

His maternal grandfather, Francis McAdam, hailed from Scotland, growing up in Musselburgh on the coast of the Firth of Forth, and Harry took much pleasure in telling his Scottish comrades and friends that he was entitled to wear the red, green and white MacGregor tartan kilt and matching tam o'shanter – not that he ever did.

He also declined trying his hand at playing the bagpipes, the music of which was sometimes featured in Salvation Army meetings, but with his poet's heart Harry admired the work of Scottish poet Robert Burns, the Bard of Ayrshire. "There was a homeliness about his poems that related to the people," he says.

As for Scottish cuisine, when Harry visited corps on Sunday to lead meetings he was invariably invited to share meals with the local comrades. Whether the meal consisted of a traditional roast dinner or cock-a-leekie soup, haggis, mince and tatties or other Scottish dishes, Harry was always grateful for the generous hospitality shown.

In June 1966, just two years after being welcomed to the South West Scotland Division, Harry and Win unexpectedly received farewell orders. When they travelled to Sunbury Court for the divisional commanders' and divisional youth secretaries' councils, Harry received word that he was to be once again appointed to the Training College.

"We enjoyed our time in Scotland very much indeed," Harry says. "I was more than pleased with the progress being made where the corps officers were enthusiastic and positive and we were building the corps and the young people's work together. It was a very rewarding and fulfilling time during which, in serving God together, lifelong friendships were made."

10

SETTING THE PACE

Progress occurs when courageous, skilful leaders seize the opportunity to change things for the better.
~ HARRY S. TRUMAN

As Major Harry Read once again approached the hallowed portals of the International Training College in June 1966, having earlier spent seven years as a sectional officer there, his enthusiasm knew no bounds. "I belonged to the college," he says. "I was almost part of the furniture, and I was looking forward to contributing to its ongoing development. I loved the college, I loved the cadets, I loved working with the staff. I had so much respect for everyone."

Harry had been appointed as field training officer, with responsibility for oversight of cadets' ministry opportunities, summer and winter assignments, partnering with corps in Sunday services, engagement with the community, and leading programmes for children and young people. Harry, Win, John and Margaret happily moved in to their allocated quarters at Herne Hill, within walking distance of the Training College in Denmark Hill.

Welcomed to the college by the training principal, Commissioner Clarence Wiseman, Harry immediately settled in to his role. In a changing world, the curriculum was becoming more progressive, with several innovations including seminars covering public relations and stewardship, and human relations and pastoral counselling courses.

On the other hand, reflecting The Salvation Army's traditional stance on married women officers at that time, Win was once again not given an appointment, despite her educational qualifications. As well as possessing a deep spirituality and an innate ability to relate to everyone she met, Win was highly intelligent. When a national newspaper featured an article and test paper from Mensa, whose members have an IQ in the top two per cent of the population, John and Margaret persuaded Win to take the test and send it away. She was surprised to receive a letter in reply asking her to visit the organisation in London with a view to following through on her excellent results, an offer she declined.

"I've always been in favour of the advancement of women officers, married or not," Harry says. "Although Win had no official appointment, she joined in the fellowship at the Nunhead Corps, two miles from our quarters, and also took on leadership of the corps cadets. It was her very gentle but nevertheless proud opportunity to build a corps cadet brigade of great value to the corps, and seven of her corps cadets eventually went to the Training College to become officers."

As for John and Margaret, with the quality of their education always a priority for Harry and Win, settling them in to new schools was one of their first concerns. John was promptly accepted at Alleyn's School in nearby Dulwich, an independent boys school established in 1882, originally called the 'College of God's gift'.

Margaret was a few months short of being eligible for high school, which put Harry and Win in rather a predicament. Within a few minutes of where they lived was the Mary Datchelor Girls School, where daughters of officers serving at the Training College had attended over the years. Harry met the headmistress, Miss Enid Goodwin, and explained the situation regarding Margaret. Because of the quality of the Salvation Army girls who attended the school, the headmistress was very fulsome, in Harry's words, and allowed Margaret to come to the school in a dress similar to the school uniform until she was of the age to formally attend.

Some time later the United Kingdom Government introduced a policy of comprehensive education, with pressure on local authorities to convert grammar schools to comprehensives, and eventually Mary Datchelor Girls School was closed. Harry received a phone call from the headmistress, who said, "We have a number of pianos here – would The Salvation Army have any use for them?" He readily accepted her generous offer and 40 well-maintained, high-quality pianos were donated to various corps who were delighted to receive them.

There was more to follow. A short time later Miss Goodwin again contacted Harry to inform him that the school had money available which, unless it was accounted for, would be appropriated by the government. He was astonished and grateful to accept on behalf of the Training College a donation of £30,000.

In the meantime, training of the first-year Messengers of the Faith and second-year Witnesses to the Faith sessions continued. With an increasing number of married cadets with children entering the college, a new nursery with an enclosed playground was provided. As field training officer for the men, Harry was also responsible for married couples, with his counterpart, Major Fleur Booth, leading the single women cadets.

Guest speakers were often invited to the college, including Gladys Aylward, a diminutive Christian missionary renowned for her courage, faith and determination, who served in China for most of her life. Her captivating story, including taking care of hundreds of orphaned children during the Sino-Japanese war, inspired a book, *The Little Woman*; a film, *The Inn of the Sixth Happiness*; and a television documentary.

Another compelling speaker was Oxford University Professor C.A. Coulson, a Christian mathematician and theoretical chemist, who spoke on the unity of science and faith. Professor Coulson was also the chair of Oxfam from 1965-1971.

Each Saturday the cadets held an open air meeting in the bustling shopping centre in nearby Camberwell. The market atmosphere of the wide main street attracted hundreds of shoppers, and in front of the shops were barrows filled with merchandise. Finding it difficult to secure a vacant spot for an open air meeting, Harry enquired about hiring a barrow and was told it was on a first come, first served basis, with those who queued up at 8 am to pay a deposit able to rent a barrow for the day. So early on Saturday morning a barrow was hired and set up with Salvation Army publications and Christian books, while at the same time securing a space for open air meetings. Harry organised shifts of cadets to attend to the barrow, and others to hold open air meetings throughout the day.

He also contacted the publishers of the Christian books that were being offered to passers-by, explaining that they were too expensive to ensure a ready sale, and mentioning what an opportunity it was for spreading the word. With the publishers' agreement, Harry was able to purchase the books at a large discount and sales significantly increased.

Harry was given permission to take the entire men's side, including their wives, to Northern Ireland for an evangelistic campaign, a huge logistical exercise in a religiously divided community. Arriving on Friday evening, during the next 10 days groups of cadets with their accompanying sectional officers held campaigns at various corps in the area. Harry travelled to different venues during the week to observe how the cadets were getting on and at the weekend took personal charge of a group of cadets.

"Campaigns I loved," Harry says. "We went to Lurgan, a large corps, and held an open air meeting in the town centre on Saturday. Afterwards we enjoyed a fine welcome meeting, followed by a pub raid. At closing time, we invited people to come to the hall for coffee and a meeting. It was well-attended – boisterous at times – and we had two seekers. Not a bad start to a campaign."

On Sunday, even though the meetings were well-attended and powerful, there were no seekers and this continued throughout the week. Harry says, "It was a massive test of faith and I made special preparations for the final Sunday morning holiness meeting. I recall majoring on the words 'Prove me now' [Malachi 3:10] and at the end of my address I placed my open Bible on the mercy seat and said, 'Here is the challenge from God: are you willing to prove him – now?' Immediately, folk started coming forward; it was so deeply moving. We closed the meeting at 1 pm. In the praise meeting at 3 pm, when the appeal was made, once again the mercy seat was lined repeatedly, as it was in the evening meeting."

The last seeker of the day was a man who had been the drummer in the corps band but after an upset occurred hadn't attended for quite some time. During the prayer meeting, after an earnest conversation with a cadet and local comrades, when he made his way to the mercy seat the congregation was overjoyed. There were 87 seekers on that Sunday.

"The cadet sergeant who had shared the leadership of the campaign returned with me in January, as per the original plan," Harry says, "to enrol the converts who made decisions during our time there. Faith is the key! Lurgan Corps is written on my heart."

Some time later, there was a large Salvation Army band festival in London and Lurgan band was on duty. When Harry greeted members of the band he was overwhelmed by their response but the warmest moment came when the drummer, now reunited with his long-discarded drum, gave him "a good Irish hug".

A change in leadership at the college saw Commissioner Herbert Westcott appointed as training principal and the further expansion of the college curriculum. The library was enlarged and the books reclassified, and visiting lecturers' subjects included marriage counselling, treatment of the mentally ill, alcoholism and drug dependency.

An external studies section of the college's education department offered wide range of courses for officers, including Salvation Army journalism and Bible study courses for discussion groups or by correspondence. College open days were also held, with attendance by the London advisory board, Salvation Army friends and representatives of local authorities.

The arrival at the college of a large cadet intake named the Evangelists, together with the second-year cadets of Messengers of the Faith, resulted in a total of 270 cadets in residence, including 42 married couples with 45 children, necessitating organisation of suitable accommodation. Provision of a car park for officers' and cadets' cars was also made.

In this his second leadership stint at the Training College, Harry once again provided the script and produced the cadets' pageants for the commissioning celebrations, the first being for the Witnesses of the Faith session, which he titled 'More Than Conquerors'. Oversighting the commissioning pageant held at the Royal Albert Hall was an assignment he was to carry out for the next seven years.

Stepping into Captain John Larsson's shoes as the composer who put Harry's words to music was Captain Robert Redhead, with whom he enjoyed a warm and collegial relationship. "When Bob was appointed to the Training College as a house officer, it was with the knowledge that because of his musical prowess he would work with me and compose the music for the commissioning pageants," Harry says.

In preparing a script for an upcoming cadets' commissioning in the Royal Albert Hall, Harry had the feeling that a special kind of song was needed but somehow the inspiration wasn't flowing. He had written a chorus but although he wrote a number of verses they never seemed quite right so he discarded them.

However, in conversation with his son John during his late teens, Harry was aware that John had moved away from his childhood faith, and "it slowly dawned on me," he says, "that the song was closer to hand than I had imagined. The Lord was leading me to John and, through him, the theme of the song became clear."

With inspiration pulsing, the verses came effortlessly, and so the song 'Become Aware of Him' was written, its tender, evocative message striking a chord with all who were to sing its poignant words:

Jesus knows your way,
The road your feet now tread;
Jesus knows your way,
The steps that lie ahead.
Far past the distant view
With dangers ever new,
He knows your way
And walks that way with you.

Chorus:
Become aware of him,
For he is ever near;
Speak out your prayer to him
For he will ever hear.
Stretch out your hand to him,
He's ever by your side;
Leave all you've planned to him
And let him guide.

Jesus knows your heart,
Those depths of hidden fire,
Jesus knows your heart,
Those heights of pure desire,
His love can scan and tell
The forces that rebel,
He knows your heart
And longs within to dwell.

Jesus knows your life
The man whom time has made;
Jesus knows your life
With all its light and shade,
Knows what you ought to be,
Sees your great destiny;
He knows your life
And offers Calvary.

"After the song was written, Bob Redhead wrote the music with his consummate skill," Harry says. "The cadets sang it wonderfully well, possibly because they too related to the theme, and it was to become part of the Army's international music ministry. Quite some time later I shared with John the source of the song and since then it's been known in our family as 'John's song.'"

In 1969 Harry received a change of appointment, once again at the Training College, to become second side officer, responsible for the domestic arrangements for men cadets and their wives. His responsibilities included oversighting their day-to-day needs, including the dining room and nursery, monitoring their health, and liaising with their house officers.

Harry also assisted the chief men's side officer, Colonel Albert Mingay, in organising, and sometimes leading, In-Sundays – intensive spiritual meetings – for cadets. It was an appointment Harry appreciated because it was less time-consuming, enabling him to spend more time writing the pageants and also undertaking additional study.

During this time Harry's mother Florence was far from well, having suffered from Parkinson's disease for a number of years. "Our Health Service did the very best for her, including two brain operations which alleviated the trembling, and we had no complaints about her treatment," Harry says.

Florence Read was promoted to Glory in June 1969 and her service of remembrance was conducted by Major Ted Cotterill, Harry's friend from their time together at Dorking, their first corps appointment as lieutenants, 20 years ago.

In 1970 Lieut-Commissioner Harry Warren was appointed as training principal and Harry was delighted to welcome him to the college.

"When I was a paratrooper, Harry Warren was the divisional youth secretary for the Tees Division in the north of England, where I come from," he says. "When my father died I was granted leave to attend his funeral. Harry also attended and was very solicitous for my mother's welling, something I appreciated so very much. From that time on, we had a warm relationship."

Once again in partnership with Robert Redhead, the song 'We Are an Army' was written for the upcoming cadets' commissioning pageant in 1971. "We would be performing on the immense Royal Albert Hall platform for verses one and three, but I had asked Bob to write the second verse to a slower tempo while a large empty cross was carried down the extensive middle aisle to the platform. It all came together rather well," Harry says.

High aloft Earth's banners fly,
In defiance of our Lord,
Christless souls his love deny,
Rampant evil takes the sword;
'Gainst the host who flout his law
God, in mercy, goes to war

Chorus:
We are an Army mobilised by God,
The cry of need our trumpet call,
We are an Army pledged to fight for God,
Until his foes before him fall.
Marching on with faith prevailing,
Marching on with hope unfailing,
Marching on with love travailing,
We are an Army, we are an Army,
Mobilised by God.

'Neath an empty cross we fight,
Love's great sacrificial sign,
Emblem of his risen might,
Token of his grace divine.
Through this cross raised up for sin,
We shall conquer, we shall win.

Christ is with us in the field,
Leaves us not to stand alone;
Evil hands the sword must yield,
Christ will make the world his own.
Loud our songs of triumph ring,
Christ is Saviour, Christ is King.

"If I have a complaint at all about the song it is that the music editorial folk changed my line in verse two to 'Through this cross raised up *by* sin' to 'Through this cross raised up *for* sin'. My point was that God took the very cross that was supposed to be the end of Christ and, therefore, his kingdom, and used it to destroy all that his enemies were defending and stood for."

While on the college staff, Harry and Win purchased their first car, paying the large sum of £25. Harry was to find that the car was a petrol-guzzler, doing only 12 miles to the gallon. However, he used it to drive to the Open University, at the time situated at Alexandra Palace in North London, where he was studying for the certificate of proficiency in religious knowledge. The Training College had a four-year study course for this subject, but with characteristic commitment Harry successfully completed the course at the Open University in just one year.

By 1972 Harry had spent another seven years at the Training College, educating and inspiring hundreds of cadets to fulfil their God-given calling. Sitting in his office one morning, when opening his mail he was surprised to receive a letter requesting him to attend International Headquarters, on a specified date and time, for an interview.

"I phoned Win straight away, telling her that we were obviously going to receive a change of appointment," Harry says. He could never have imagined what that appointment would be – it was to take his life and service as a Salvation Army officer in an entirely new direction.

11

SPREADING THE NEWS

Faith comes from hearing the message, and the message is heard through the word about Christ.

~ ROMANS 10:17

Arriving at International Headquarters in good time for his scheduled meeting, Harry was ushered into the office of Colonel Frank Hutchings, assistant to the Chief of the Staff, Commissioner Arnold Brown. After a few minutes of affable chatting, Colonel Hutchings said, "I hope you're happy with your new appointment," to which Harry replied with a smile, "I'm sure I will be when you tell me what it is."

When the colonel informed him that his appointment was as press officer and director of Information Services in succession to Major Will Pratt, Harry was almost lost for words. After a moment's pause, he said, "That's interesting … I have no experience in that field." Colonel Hutchings assured Harry that he was expected to do well in his new appointment, with good reason.

Articulate and astute, with an engaging personality and quick wit, he was soon to become an excellent media ambassador for The Salvation Army, with its message of preaching the gospel of Jesus Christ and meeting human needs in his name without discrimination. "It was an important job, and paid rich dividends in the end," Harry says.

Strongly advocating for Win to also work in Information Services, he stood his ground when the answer was, "Wives don't do that kind of task with their husbands." "Well, let there be a first time," he insisted, "I would like my wife to be a member of staff." His quiet insistence ensured that Win worked in the department, to great effect. "Win knew how to handle difficult situations and people. She was careful not to tread on people's toes and always got the best out of them," Harry says.

The change of appointment came with a minimum of family upheaval. When Harry had been appointed as second side officer at the Training College, they had moved from Herne Hill to Grove Lane, Camberwell, next to the college. With Harry's appointment as press officer he, Win and Margaret remained in the quarters where they had lived for the past three years. John was at this time a student at Teachers Training College in Bishops Stortford, and Margaret was still at school.

In his very first day at the office, within hours of beginning work, Harry was to undergo a proverbial baptism of fire. He and Win were taking a break for morning tea when the Editorial Department's photographer, an employee named Laurie, strode in, slapped a copy of a leading newspaper on the table and said, "Someone's got to answer for this!" Life as press officer, Harry realised, involved quick thinking, decisiveness and a readiness to immediately respond in an appropriate way to breaking news.

In an investigative journalism article, the newspaper reported that during an undercover surveillance of a Salvation Army hostel for homeless men it was discovered that entry to a night-time card school on the premises was by a bottle of wine, much against the teetotal rules of the Army and the hostel. The article didn't pull any punches and, as the newly-appointed press officer, it was up to Harry to resolve the situation.

He immediately contacted the Army's Social Services Department who confirmed that the story was accurate but the reason the incident had happened was because the officer-in-charge was in hospital after having been attacked by one of the men. "We entrusted one of our workers to take charge while the officer was in hospital and he had allowed this to happen."

Harry phoned the newspaper office, asking to speak to the editor, and was put straight through. "Good morning," he said, addressing the editor by name. "Regarding the story about the Salvation

Army hostel, your reporter got it right but it is true only because the person who would have been responsible was in hospital being treated for injuries inflicted by one of the men at the hostel." Choosing his words carefully, Harry added, "Could I ask you to please give the same prominence to reporting the reason for the incident as you did to the initial account in your newspaper?" The editor paused for a moment before courteously answering, "I will do that for you, Mr Read."

As he settled in to the job, Harry was delighted to have as his assistant Captain Jenty Fairbank, whose experience and skill he greatly appreciated. Later in her officership Jenty became a well-known Salvation Army author and historian. When she shared with Harry that she had long felt a call to serve in Africa, he strongly encouraged her to pursue that calling. Eventually serving as a lecturer at Howard Teacher Training College in Zimbabwe, Africa, after a number of years Jenty was herself appointed as press officer at International Headquarters.

Harry soon made himself known to diverse media outlets, including newspaper editors and reporters and radio and television organisations. From the beginning of his officership, Harry aspired at all times to foster warm personal relationships with whoever he was working with. Following this precept as press officer, his thoughtful, gracious personality endeared him to – and was appreciated by – the sometimes world-weary media press corps.

Also strongly embedded in Harry's life and work, regardless of his appointment, was his pastoral care as a Salvation Army officer. "I recall that I was missing one of the reporters who had been at various press conferences," Harry says. "I obtained his home phone number and his wife was deeply moved that I was enquiring after him, as he was seriously ill. Experiences such as this made my time in the Information Services so very fulfilling and fruitful."

As director of Information Services, in cooperation with the Public Relations and Chief of the Staff departments, Harry's was a pivotal role in the 1970s, a time which saw a marked increase in The Salvation Army's public witness through the media.

The first reported broadcast of a Salvation Army programme on radio was in 1923 when Govan (Scotland) Band played in a Glasgow studio. Fifty years later, on Palm Sunday 1973, it was estimated that a total of 20 million listeners in Britain heard three Salvation Army broadcasts on that day – the BBC People's Service in the morning, the ITV programme *Stars on Sunday* at 7 pm, and at 7.30 a half-hour of community hymn singing accompanied by the Upper Norwood Band.

During his time as press officer, Harry enjoyed a lively and convivial association with Commissioner Catherine Bramwell-Booth, the eldest daughter of General Bramwell Booth and Florence Soper Booth, and granddaughter of founders William and Catherine Booth. He was not alone in his admiration of this sprightly lady.

Because of her warm disposition, impeccable diction and sharp mind, Catherine Bramwell-Booth became a sought-after media personality in her nineties, making frequent appearances on radio and television. During the 1970s and '80s she was interviewed, among others, by Malcolm Muggeridge, Russell Harty, and Roy Plomley on *Desert Island Discs*.

Commissioner Catherine also appeared on *Parkinson*, a top-rating television show hosted by Michael Parkinson, who was later to be knighted by the Queen. During their chat she mentioned that she would very much like to live to the age of 100. "Commissioner, my money's on you," said Parkinson, to which she replied with mock severity, "I hope you're not a betting man!", prompting peals of laughter from the audience.

Parky was captivated, asserting, "Catherine Bramwell-Booth was quite the most remarkable woman I have ever met, and [in a career spanning more than 40 years] I've met a few." High praise indeed! Catherine Bramwell-Booth celebrated her 100th birthday in 1983, the year she was honoured with the Order of the Founder.

"Because of the commissioner's increasing popularity with the media," Harry says, "it was decided my office would be the link between her and the broadcasters in order to protect her from any media hassle. So I became a reasonably frequent visitor to the home

Commissioner Catherine shared with her sisters, Colonel Olive and Major Dora. For me, each visit was a special occasion."

On Harry's arrival, the redoubtable Commissioner Catherine would look at him kindly, posing the question, "And how are you in your soul, Major?" After his reassurances, she would ask about the spiritual wellbeing of his family, an interest that never failed to bless and impress him.

On one occasion the Press Association organised a filmed conversation with Commissioner Catherine and other well-known church leaders in the large lounge room of her home. In due time she made her stately way downstairs wearing her large, old-fashioned bonnet, and the film director whispered to Harry, "We can't see her face clearly because of her bonnet. Can you get her to take it off?"

With all the diplomacy he could muster, Harry asked Commissioner Catherine to go back upstairs and take her bonnet off. When she returned minus the iconic bonnet she invariably wore for media appearances, she was almost unrecognisable. Realising his mistake, the director asked Harry, "Can you get her to put her bonnet on again?" Smiling at the memory, Harry says, "I think the bravest and most successful thing I ever did in my life was to persuade Commissioner Catherine to go back up to her room and return once again wearing her bonnet."

Although Harry was virtually on call 24/7 because of the relentless anything-can-happen-at-any-time news cycle, there were days where time could be spent in happy fellowship with other officers and staff. In his retirement, General Frederick Coutts had an office at International Headquarters because he was doing a fair amount of writing. If anything stirred him in the UK press, or if he was restless from time to time in the confines of his small office and needed someone to talk to, he would pop down to Harry's office for a chat. "I was always a great fan of his and learned much from him," Harry says.

Another visitor was Captain Howard Davies, who had recently arrived from Australia to work in the International Music Editorial

Department with Captain Robert Redhead. Calling in to the Public Relations Department, Howard Davies was introduced to Harry. "I have never forgotten how warmly Harry Read greeted me," Howard says in his memoir *Words and Music*. "It was as if we had been friends for decades rather than meeting for the first time. Over the four decades since then I have had the pleasure of setting several of his thought-provoking lyric-verses to music."

Six months into Harry's appointment, on 8 March 1973, he took a phone call from the Army's Emergency Services with the shocking news that the Provisional IRA had detonated a bomb outside the Old Bailey Courthouse in London, the first major attack since the Troubles began in the 1960s. The Salvation Army was quickly on the scene to render assistance to the scores of casualties and, as the Old Bailey was in the vicinity of International Headquarters, Harry made his way there. The area was cordoned off but when the police saw his Army uniform he was immediately waved through. "There were so many tributes to The Salvation Army and their assistance at this distressing time was greatly appreciated," Harry says.

With the publication in 1974 of *In Darkest England Now*, a sequel to William Booth's *In Darkest England and the Way Out*, a press conference was organised, attended by General Erik Wickberg who had written the foreword. Published by Hodder & Stoughton, *In Darkest England Now*, lengthily subtitled *A Salvation Army survey of religious and social conditions in Britain eighty years after William Booth's blueprint for salvation*, depicted how changes in society had affected the work of The Salvation Army, which prompted much interest and discussion.

Soon afterwards, with the impending retirement of General Wickberg, a High Council was called to elect his successor. Beginning on Saturday 4 May 1974 at historic Sunbury Court, the High Council was attended by 40 Salvation Army leaders from around the world. Harry was delegated to generate the interest of the media and to organise their coverage of the event. He was also responsible for the definitive film of the High Council that year.

The international leaders were welcomed by Queen Elizabeth,

the Queen Mother, at a reception at St James's Palace. They were also given a public welcome at Westminster Central Hall. As the High Council got underway, members who accepted nomination were Commissioners Arnold Brown, Geoffrey Dalziel, Paul Kaiser and Clarence Wiseman. At 4.30 pm on 13 May, Commissioner Clarence Wiseman, the territorial commander for Canada and Bermuda, and a self-confessed "incurable Salvationist", was announced as the 10th General of The Salvation Army.

As Harry had established a dynamic working relationship with members of the media, Sunbury Court was inundated with reporters and photographers on the final day of proceedings. With deadlines to meet, they were watching the clock awaiting the outcome, and when the announcement was made there was a flurry of activity, with Harry on hand to assist wherever needed.

During the next few months, Harry received many requests from the media to interview General Wiseman and he expected that the General would have an officer delegated to transport him to such appointments. "To my surprise that was not so," Harry says, "and I said to him, 'General, I don't have a wonderfully smart car but if I put myself and my car at your disposal to take you to these appointments I will consider it to be an honour.' The General readily agreed to that arrangement."

On one occasion General Wiseman and his wife, Mrs General Janet Wiseman, were invited to lunch with Queen Elizabeth II at Buckingham Palace, along with a number of Salvation Army officers including Harry and Win, an honour they very much enjoyed. "The Queen has a gentle way of expressing warmth and normality at the same time," Harry says. "She is the epitome of wisdom and graciousness. The Duke of Edinburgh, on the other hand, welcomed everyone with a big smile on his face and enjoyed a bit of repartee. The Queen Mother was also present and charmed everyone."

General Wiseman also attended the enthronement of Dr Donald Coggan as the 101st Archbishop of Canterbury, the first Salvation Army General to be so invited. As Archbishop-Designate Dr Coggan had accompanied General Wiseman on a late-night visit to those sleeping rough in central London, helping to load The Salvation Army's van with hot soup and bread. It was a visit they would both long remember.

Among other high-profile dignitaries to have a warm association with The Salvation Army was Prime Minister Harold Wilson, who had been elected to that office in 1974. Harry and other Salvation Army representatives were invited on separate occasions to the Houses of Parliament and a private meeting at 10 Downing Street where the prime minister expressed his appreciation and thanks for the work of The Salvation Army. He also accepted an invitation to speak at an officers' councils.

One of the media representatives Harry resonated particularly well with was a member of the BBC Religious Department, an Anglican minister who organised a Sunday morning radio programme on BBC Radio 2. The minister told Harry that, in trying to modernise the programme to attract younger people, older listeners had become alienated and ratings had dropped.

"In discussion we came to the conclusion," Harry says, "that we could produce a programme of Salvation Army music with broad appeal for audiences of all ages." With the support of Army musicians including Major Les Condon, a programme with the catchy title of *Banners and Bonnets* was devised.

The programme was presented by Ray Moore, a genial and talented British broadcaster who went on to become a household name in the 1980s, presenting his top-rating early morning show on BBC Radio 2 with five and quarter million listeners. "When I met with Ray Moore and told him what we had in mind he was very happy to accept," Harry says, "and as we worked through each programme together we related really well right from the beginning." Harry, Ray and his wife Alma became lifelong friends.

Banners and Bonnets was a great success, described by the BBC as "a lively miscellany of Salvation Army music". The programme alternated with *Gospel Road*, hosted by top-selling singer Cliff Richard, and a Welsh programme called *Come Alive*, at 8 am on Sundays, on BBC2.

More sombre news was to be reported when, at 8.46 am on 28 February 1975 a London underground train crashed into a concrete wall at the end of a tunnel at Moorgate station. Forty-three people died and 86 were injured. *BBC News* reported, "The rescue operation has involved several teams – London Underground staff, fire crews, doctors and nurses from St Bartholomew's Hospital and members of The Salvation Army. They have been working all day to free the dead and the injured from the tangled mass of metal in atrocious conditions."

Under the leadership of Major Joe Burlison of The Salvation Army's Emergency Services, an area was set up on Platform 11 where rescuers could take a break and be served a cup of tea. Women in the team were bathing sore eyes and using cotton buds to remove soot from ears and noses of the rescuers. Harry was full of praise for Joe Burlison, describing him as "indefatigable and resourceful – everything you would look for in a man who was representing The Salvation Army in such demanding circumstances".

The Army's team resolutely remained at the scene until midday on the following Wednesday, 5 March. Three weeks after the disaster, when the relief workers were invited to a reception at 10 Downing Street, Prime Minister Harold Wilson commented, "We took it for granted that The Salvation Army would be there."

When well-earned holidays came around, Harry and Win often went to Mexborough to stay with Win's mother and catch up with family and friends. Ever industrious, even on furlough, Harry "took work on holiday", keeping his pen and notepaper handy to jot down plans and inspirations. "There was no hardship in it," he says. However, when their visit happened to coincide with a Test match at Sheffield, just a half hour's drive from Mexborough, he enjoyed sitting in the stands and cheering England on.

One morning in August 1975 Harry was not at his desk as usual, having advised his staff that he would be late that day. It was Harry and Win's great pleasure to take Margaret to the International Training College, where she was to be Cadet Margaret Read of the Companions of Christ session for the next two years. Margaret having been an accepted candidate, they had looked forward to this day for quite some time. As they drew up in the familiar grounds of the college where Harry had served for some 15 years in three separate appointments, he and Win were full of joy. “We couldn't have been more proud,” Harry says.

Soon afterwards, following three eventful years as press officer and director of Information Services, another change of appointment was in the offing for Harry and Win. Their strong preference was to be again appointed as corps officers. In a meeting with British Commissioner Geoffrey Dalziel, Harry was told by his good friend that he and Win would be going to Nottingham, the birthplace of William Booth, not as corps officers but as divisional leaders.

12

TAKING THE LEAD

My arms are around the world; my heart is set upon its salvation.

~ WILLIAM BOOTH

Welcomed to the Nottingham Division in early November 1975, Harry and Win were greeted by hundreds of Salvationists and local dignitaries who had gathered in the Great Hall of the Nottingham Conference Centre as the William Booth Memorial Hall lacked sufficient seating for such a large crowd. The joyous proceedings and many warm words of welcome augured well for their appointment as divisional leaders.

With his experience in public relations, Harry had prepared well for his introduction to Nottingham, drafting a media release to be sent out by the division before his arrival, outlining his service in The Salvation Army and expressing his vision for the future. In the days after his arrival he was inundated with requests for media interviews.

High on the list of recommended places to visit in the City of Nottingham is the William Booth Birthplace Museum, situated at 12 Notintone Place, Sneinton, built in 1914-1915 to honour the memory of the founder of The Salvation Army. At the front of the museum a statue of William Booth stands on a pedestal with his right hand raised in The Salvation Army salute. A plaque above the entrance reads: "In this house was born on 10th April 1829 William Booth Founder and General of The Salvation Army".

As the newly-appointed divisional commander and divisional home league secretary of the Nottingham Division, Harry and Win may have well expected their Divisional Headquarters to do justice to the historic locale with such significance for the worldwide Salvation Army. However, they were to find that was far from the case.

The Nottingham Divisional Headquarters was located in three rooms of the small Aspley Green Corps in a suburb of Nottingham. Such was the setup that when home league or other meetings were held at the corps on weekdays Divisional Headquarters staff were confined to their offices.

Just before Harry left International Headquarters, Queen Elizabeth II had responded in a very powerful way to a problem that had arisen and this was reported by the media. Appreciating the Queen's reaffirmation of her own Christian point of view on this matter, Harry wrote to her thanking her for her stance. When a letter from Buckingham Palace in reply, addressed to Major Harry Read and forwarded from International Headquarters, arrived at Divisional Headquarters the place was abuzz. "The divisional commander's got a letter from the Queen!" they said. How could they fail to be impressed by their new leader?

Harry enjoyed Win's presence in the office as divisional home league secretary. He also enjoyed warm friendships with the divisional youth secretary, Captain Keith Banks, and Keith's wife Pauline, who had once been a member of the Joystrings, "a remarkable lady whose assistance in the division was greatly appreciated". As for his personal assistant, Joan Cuthbert, Harry is full of praise, declaring that she was one of the best secretaries he ever had.

The Nottingham Division consisted of approximately 50 corps, with many of the corps officers having been cadets under Harry's direction during his time at the Training College. Harry and Win's pastoral hearts were also evidenced as divisional leaders. "We had warm relationships with all the officers," Harry says. He was surprised, and more than a little perturbed, to find that some officers had an additional corps under their direction, with a few being responsible for three corps in total.

During their welcome meeting at Divisional Headquarters, Harry and Win were enjoying a cup of tea and cream cakes provided by the staff when the phone rang, with the caller asking to speak to the divisional commander. Harry took the call from a rather distressed lady who informed him that her corps officer had told her the corps was closing from that day's date. When Harry checked with Keith Banks, he was told, "How on earth can we close that corps? We're spending a small fortune on a new young people's hall there."

Harry lost no time in telling the lady that the meetings would be held at the corps on Sunday at the usual time, led by the officer. He then contacted the corps officer and said, "You are doing something that I'm not allowed to do," adding with some vigour, "whatever arrangements you make, please look after that corps until we sort things out," a directive the corps officer complied with.

After praying and pondering about his divisional leadership, Harry formulated a plan for the future. Realising that the Nottingham Division was naturally made up of four geographical parts, with corps in each vicinity, he grouped the corps officers into four sections. Each group of officers in turn was invited to Divisional Headquarters for a meeting. "Bring your Bible," Harry told them, "I would like to talk to you about an immediate problem."

Discussion centred around the fact that the division had some corps with no officers, some with inadequate premises and some that were struggling to maintain their programmes, with declining numbers attending. "We wanted to harness the power of prayer," Harry says, "so we started a divisional prayer circle with officers and soldiers." Harry also enlisted the help of Lieut-Colonel Grace McCorgal, a retired assistant field secretary, who coordinated the response to the division's plans for its future direction, with gratifying results.

A number of Salvationists who offered to be envoys, that is non-commissioned officers, were carefully interviewed, vetted and approved, eventually taking charge of a corps, and this was a remarkably successful initiative. "A couple of corps were closed but other corps got their fair measure of independence," Harry says. "It was a real answer to prayer." To add to the sense of God-given accomplishment, that year Captain Keith Banks, on behalf of the Nottingham

Division, farewelled 13 young Salvationists to the Training College.

Another innovation Harry made was that each Friday he and Win would travel to a designated part of the division, visiting the corps officers in turn for two or three hours and staying overnight with one of the officer couples. Sometimes their visit would coincide with a local officers' gathering at the corps. They would meet with more officers on Saturday morning before returning home in the afternoon in readiness for their leadership of the meetings at a selected corps on Sunday.

When Harry and Win were staying overnight at one of the officers' quarters, the corps officer took a phone call and, not knowing that Harry was within earshot, said, "In the morning we're meeting with the census board and we're going to ask to take quite a few people off the roll."

When officially advised of this at the census board meeting, Harry declared that he would personally write to each person whose name was mentioned, assuring them of the love and care being shown for them. He also proposed a prayer group at the corps, specifically to pray for those on the list and for the rebuilding of the fellowship.

What strange, mysterious powers there are in prayer!
A motivated person kneels to pray,
And to his Lord confesses his deep care,
With childlike faith, he finds the words to say,

And forces stored in heaven are released
To do their work in heart and circumstance,
Momentum gathers, righteousness increased,
And God's great Army sees a new advance.

Through prayer we harness God's great power,
By faith, creation's energy employ,
Observe how care and prayer begin to flower,
And witness pain and loss turn into joy.

Those who learn by faith to intercede
Work with the Lord to meet great human need.

A few months later Harry and Win led the Sunday meetings at the corps, and Harry presented commissions to three uniformed Salvationists, rejoicing that these people were among those proposed to be taken off the roll. "It was a time of great growth in the division and we gave thanks to God," he says.

During this time a representative from International Headquarters came to the division to present the corps officers with plans to introduce stewardship, defined as "a product of a life surrendered to God, knowing that everything we own is God's and we are here on earth to manage it". More than financial giving, stewardship is a whole-of-life commitment. "It isn't just a case of giving more in our cartridge, it is having a big vision and the courage to see it through," Harry says. "In the initial stages some corps officers seemed reluctant, but with faith and commitment the challenge to introduce stewardship was successful."

The witness of bands and songsters in presenting the gospel message was an important part of Salvation Army comradeship in the division, with the Nottingham William Booth Memorial Halls band the fourth oldest in the Army and the Nottingham songster brigade formed more than a century ago. At the same time Harry was keen to promote what he terms grassroots Salvationism, encouraging corps officers to inspire their comrades to meet community needs including league of mercy hospital visitation and tending to the lonely, bereaved, poor and needy.

In 1975 a young man named Dick Krommenhoek was commissioned to start a pop group in the Netherlands Territory. Naming the group Grace, Dick wrote the music for three songs, but was unsure about who would write the words. The bandmaster of the Amsterdam Staff Band from 1976-1981, a Yorkshireman by the name of Major Maurice Cooper, suggested he contact Major Harry Read.

"As divisional commander I was exceedingly hard pressed," Harry says, "but I wrote the three songs Dick wanted and we've been friends ever since." One of the songs written is titled 'Jesus', and the refrain of this song is unforgettably beautiful:

As a wing is to a bird,
As breath is to a word,
As a melody gives life to a song,
Is my Jesus all day long.

Harry was instrumental in Dick and his wife Vibeke being accepted into the International Training College in 1981.

A priority for Harry as divisional commander was fostering good relationships with the Nottingham Division advisory board, which included influential businesspeople in the community, including the lord mayor. He was always happy and proud to escort the board members – and any visitors to the division – to the William Booth Birthplace Museum where he recounted the revolutionary beginnings of The Salvation Army. The board members were warmly appreciative of the work of The Salvation Army in the area, and their assistance and advice was an important contribution to the continuation of the Army's service.

"We loved Nottingham because of its history," Harry says, "and the standing of The Salvation Army in the community had to be seen to be believed." Typical of the amenability shown by benefactors was the rental of a hall on the fringe of the business district of Nottingham to a local corps for just one shilling per annum. However, after a number of years, the generous businessman decided that he wanted to adapt the hall for commercial purposes and advised Divisional Headquarters that he wished to rescind the agreement.

Harry discussed the situation with the advisory board, stating earnestly, "I have said my prayers about this and I feel that we should purchase the property ourselves rather than surrender it to be used commercially." One of the board members, who was well versed in property management, asked, "How strongly do you feel about this, Harry?" "I feel exceedingly convinced about this," Harry replied, "I feel the usefulness of this property to the work of The Salvation Army is too big an asset for us to lose."

The answer came unexpectedly, unanimously and immediately:

"We will undertake as an advisory board to buy the freehold so that The Salvation Army can continue to operate there." In due course finance was canvassed from wealthy donors and the property was kept for the use of Army.

One of the advisory board members was a prominent member of the Nottingham County Cricket Club and, with an interest in cricket being one of Harry's few diversions in his busy life, he was more than pleased to be invited to the cricket club at Trent Bridge, a world-famous cricketing landmark, where he was given the warmest of welcomes.

He also got to know Brian Clough, a famous football player, manager of Nottingham Forest Football Club and fellow Yorkshireman, who had great respect for The Salvation Army. Outspoken and often controversial, Brian Clough was dubbed "the greatest manager England never had". Harry recalls that on one occasion when a team visiting Nottingham Forest began singing a rather raunchy song, Brian Clough grabbed the microphone and announced, "Gentlemen, we do not sing that kind of song here."

Harry was among local bishops and heads of other churches who were invited to meet Queen Elizabeth II and the Duke of Edinburgh at a reception on a royal visit to Nottingham. After shaking hands with the Queen, Harry was greeted by the Duke of Edinburgh. Recognising Harry's Salvation Army uniform, Prince Phillip with characteristic banter said to him, "What are you doing here with this lot? I thought you would have been converting them!"

In one of their rare afternoons off, Harry and Win visited Sherwood Forest, home to folklore hero Robin Hood and his band of merry men – "feared by the bad, loved by the good", according to the 20th century song. Legend has it that Robin Hood and his men stole from the rich and gave to the poor, all the while being pursued by their arch enemy, the Sheriff of Nottingham. A major attraction in the forest is the 1000-year-old Major Oak, a giant, gnarled oak tree with a canopy spread of 28 metres. "You couldn't live in Nottingham and not go on a visit to Sherwood Forest," Harry says, "it's in the folk history of our nation."

On the home front, Harry and Win were delighted when John became engaged to Anne Tribble in 1975. John and Anne first met when he was working as an occupational therapist in the rehabilitation unit at The Salvation Army's Spa Road Men's Hostel, having been offered the job by the manager, Anne's father, Major Derrick Tribble.

Harry and Win and Anne's parents, Derrick and Betty, were good friends and it was in answer to their combined prayers – and also as John saw the lives of men in the hostel being transformed after they gave their lives to Christ – that his childhood faith was rekindled and he prayerfully rededicated his life to God.

It was a real family affair when John and Anne, who was given away by her father, were married in full Salvation Army uniform at Nunhead Corps on 17 July 1976, with Harry conducting the wedding. Though he had not written it at the time, Harry's poem, titled 'This Wedding Day' – an ode to the delights of Christian love – would have been a beautiful addition to the ceremony:

A wedding day is spun from dreams,
Its thread as light as gossamer,
Its pattern bright with God-blessed beams,
Its loveliness beyond compare.

The first dream is togetherness,
The thrill of touch that never fades,
The shared delights of tenderness,
Which every thought and act pervades.

There is the dream marked 'evermore',
Of marriage that will ever stand,
With God himself the guarantor
As you obey love's blessed command.

This is the dream that God has given.
He wills for you all he knows best –
That your new home reflects his Heaven,
With Christ your constant marriage guest.

Soon after their marriage John and Anne offered themselves as candidates for officership, following in the footsteps of their parents. Harry, Win, Derrick and Betty were delighted when they entered the International Training College as cadets of the Joyful Evangelists session in September 1977.

A few months earlier, with Margaret's two years at the Training College coming to an end, Harry and Win were looking forward to her commissioning as a member of the Companions of Christ session. How proud they were when, on 27 May, Lieutenant Margaret Read was commissioned in the Royal Albert Hall, along with other members of her session.

It was another joyous occasion when, just 15 days later on Saturday 11 June, Margaret walked down the aisle of the Nunhead Salvation Army Hall on the arm of her father, to be wed to Lieutenant Graham Grayston, with the service conducted by Major John Gowans.

Margaret met Graham at a youth councils weekend when she was a student at Teachers Training College in Newcastle upon Tyne and he was a newly commissioned Salvation Army officer at Alnwick. They fell in love and in those days Graham first had to ask his divisional commander for permission to 'correspond' with Margaret. Their courtship was given tacit approval when, just before Margaret went to the Training College, Graham was appointed to St Mary Cray Corps in South London, enabling them to keep in close contact for the next two years.

Graham was no stranger to the Read family, having been a cadet in the 1971-72 Blood and Fire session at the Training College when Harry was second side officer, added to which they were kindred Yorkshiremen. From the outset, Graham was a much-loved member of the family.

In the third year of Harry and Win's leadership at Nottingham, they discussed with divisional staff plans for the upcoming soldiers' rally weekend, an annual highlight for Salvationists and friends. The chief secretary, Colonel Francy Cachelin, was invited to preside over the Saturday night festival, a joyous occasion held in the biggest hall in town and featuring bands, songsters and soloists.

To their surprise, they were informed that General Arnold Brown and British Commissioner Geoffrey Dalziel would also be present. "Because of my experience in the press office," Harry says, "I knew how to get the ear of the media in Nottingham and I arranged interviews beforehand for the General and his wife and the British Commissioner and his wife. They were kept very busy."

During the festival General Brown was leading a well-known Salvation Army chorus and on the spur of the moment called Commissioner Geoffrey Dalziel and Harry to the microphone, asking them to sing the chorus as a duet. "Geoff is six foot something and I'm five foot something," Harry says with a smile, "and there was a lot of fun about our singing together."

After the duettists had delighted the congregation, the General asked Commissioner Dalziel to be seated. Standing beside Harry, General Brown outlined his years of service before announcing, "Ladies and gentlemen, meet Lieut-Colonel Harry Read." Knowing that an edict had previously been issued that no divisional commander would hold a rank above major, Harry stood rather nonplussed as he smilingly acknowledged the applause of the capacity crowd.

After the meeting Harry sought out Commissioner Dalziel, who in reply to Harry's obvious question about his promotion to Lieut-Colonel replied, "It means you'll be leaving us – you'll be going to an International Headquarters appointment." "Can you tell me a little more?" Harry asked. And the answer was, "You are to be appointed as principal of the International Training College."

After three memorable years in the Nottingham Division, Harry and Win were on the move again.

13

PRINCIPAL PRIORITIES

The wise in heart are called discerning, and gracious words promote instruction.

~ PROVERBS 16:21

Thirty-one years after arriving at the International Training College as a fresh-faced 23-year-old, Lieut-Colonel Harry Read returned as principal in June 1978, declaring that the college was "in his blood". After serving for one year in 1948-49 as a cadet sergeant, seven-and-a-half years as sectional officer in the '50s, and six years as field training officer and second side officer in the '60s and early '70s, his reception at the Training College was like a welcome home.

Directly responsible to General Arnold Brown and the Chief of the Staff, Commissioner Stanley Cottrill, Harry quickly settled in to the familiar surroundings of the college. As always, he was up bright and early each morning, beginning work well before 8 am, and working until late in the day. Harry also ensured that Win's empathy and educational expertise were fully utilised. In addition to administrative responsibilities at the college, she was also a tutor in Bible studies.

Keeping it all in the family, Harry and Win were delighted to welcome John and Anne back to the college for their second year of training in the Joyful Evangelists session. "Sometimes they would come and have a cup of tea in the office with Win and me," Harry says, "and would happily share their perspective of college life with us. They appreciated the fact that we were there."

On arriving at Denmark Hill, Harry and Win temporarily lived in an apartment on the top floor of the college, feeling right at home. "Win and I loved the college building with its years of history, and we enjoyed the fellowship of living in the same building as the cadets and members of staff," he says. Soon afterwards, they moved into a house in Forest Hill, not far from the college, and attended Nunhead as their home corps.

Always up for a challenge, Harry had his work cut out as training principal. As well as the spiritual and practical oversight of the numerous officer staff and almost 200 cadets, including many from around the international Salvation Army world, he had been specifically charged with initiating a ground-breaking operational change at the college.

Since the first Salvation Army Training Home was established in 1880, men and women cadets had been trained separately. However, after decades of segregated classes, mixed classes were introduced for the subjects generated by the college's education department, including Bible study, Salvation Army doctrine, Orders and Regulations and subject notes, i.e. preparation for sermons. It is not clear at what point these changes were introduced but that system was certainly in operation for the first full sessions after World War II.

Harry was assigned to bring together the men's and women's sides for administration, pastoral, practical and field training, so that all aspects of their cadetship would be unified.

"I was told by leadership that I would be at the college for a number of years because of the complexity of the change," Harry says. "I had to ensure that the new system was harmonious and that if there were any problems with changes of appointment – the replication of men's and women's side officers, second side officers, field officers etc. meant some officers would be moved to new appointments – those problems would be wisely yet at the same time firmly dealt with." It was a task that required much prayer, planning, diplomacy and equanimity.

After a year of planning and preparation, the amalgamation of the men's and women's training programme commenced on 1 June 1979, with God's Soldiers session being the first to experience the combined programme, and the Proclaimers of Salvation returning to the new situation for their second year of training. The innovation was hailed as not only a success but also a progressive step forward.

The Salvation Army's International Training College certainly lived up to its name at this time, welcoming cadets from many overseas countries including India, Africa, South America, Scandinavia and France, all warmly welcomed into the fellowship of the college and benefiting from the training they received before returning to serve in their home country.

Rivalling Harry in the number of years served at the Training College was the assistant principal, Lieut-Colonel Mary Carby, who was a member of the 1948 Peacemakers session when Harry was a cadet sergeant. Mary Carby returned to the college in 1959, and remained there in various appointments for a total of 22 years.

"Mary Carby, Win and I were very good friends," Harry says. "She was one of the first in our country as an officer to obtain professional qualifications in social work and she brought that expertise to her work at the Training College."

Soon after Harry and Win arrived at the college, the fifth International Congress of The Salvation Army was held in London from 30 June to 9 July, celebrating the centenary of the Army's name and the registering of the Army's 11 articles of doctrine.

Well-known to Salvationists is the story of how William Booth, when reviewing printer's proofs of the Christian Mission's 1878 report, read the words "The Christian Mission is a volunteer army", and in a moment of divine inspiration struck out the word 'volunteer' and replaced it with the word 'salvation', sparking a Christian revolution.

Designated by General Arnold Brown as "the greatest-ever convocation of Salvationists", the congress posters proclaimed "London will be invaded by Salvationists from 82 countries". Harry and Win were photographed with the General, his wife and other Salvation Army leaders at a huge open air rally held in Trafalgar Square.

It was reported that more than 30,000 people attended the 120 events held during the congress. One of those events featured Dick Krommenhoek and Grace pop group from the Netherlands, whose repertoire included 'Jesus', the song for which Harry had recently provided the words.

The cadets of the Training College participated in various congress events, and Harry was also responsible for facilitating a social conference and a missionary conference, both held at the college as part of the congress proceedings.

In another innovation, prior to Harry's return to the Training College, General Arnold Brown directed that the revised wording of the cadets' commissioning statement would be: "I commission you as an officer of The Salvation Army and *ordain* you as a minister of Christ and his gospel." This confirmed the status of officers as ordained ministers of religion, which was thought to be helpful in an international context.

During the commissioning and ordination service of the Joyful Evangelists session in the Royal Albert Hall, Harry had the pleasure of announcing the names of the cadets, including John and Anne, before they saluted the Chief of the Staff, Commissioner Cottrill, who commissioned and ordained them. Harry and Win and, of course, Derrick and Betty Tribble, were delighted when John and Anne were appointed as lieutenants to the Gateshead Corps.

With his previous experience in directing numerous commissioning pageants at the Training College, it was no surprise that, as principal, Harry took a great interest in the ongoing inspiration to be had from these presentations, deputising suitable officers to take charge of the highly anticipated events. "It certainly wasn't a question of interfering but I let them have the benefit of my experience," he says.

Harry's time as training principal coincided with more than a few significant celebrations. On 8 July 1979 special meetings were held to mark the Golden Jubilee of the opening of the William Booth Memorial Training College at Denmark Hill by HRH Prince George, with General Bramwell Booth, in his last public act, laying the cornerstone.

Designed by Sir Giles Gilbert Scott as a monument to General William Booth, with the initials W.B. emblazoned above the entrance, the extensive brick building has been listed as Grade II on the National Heritage List for England. The college also houses the library, archives and International Heritage Centre.

During the 50 years since the college's opening in 1929, more than 9000 men and women from around the world had been trained and commissioned, fulfilling their God-given calling to become Salvation Army officers, and continuing the vision of William and Catherine Booth.

In a meeting with Harry before the celebrations, General Brown advised him of his plans for the installation of a lighted stainless steel cross on the north face of the Training College tower, high above the entrance. Harry thought it was a brilliant idea, saying to himself, "'Why on earth didn't I think of that?' A lighted cross would represent our Christian faith and mission and become the focal point of the building."

During the Golden Jubilee meetings, General Brown launched an appeal to raise funds for the cross. The plan was that if the Training College raised a specified amount for the project, International Headquarters would match that amount to make up the total cost. Harry was happy to take responsibility for the college's fund-raising efforts.

A few weeks prior to this occasion, on 4 May 1979, Harry and Win were overjoyed to become grandparents for the first time when Margaret and Graham welcomed the birth of a baby boy, who they named Michael. As the new parents were corps officers at Crawley Corps, less than an hour's drive from Denmark Hill, Harry and Win were able to visit from time to time and enjoy the newest addition to the family.

They were doubly blessed when, four months later, John and Anne welcomed a baby girl, Joanna, on 25 September. John and Anne were at that time the officers at Gateshead in the north-east of England, unfortunately 300 miles and a six-hour car journey from the college.

In yet another auspicious Training College event, the centenary of the first training of Salvation Army officers at two small training homes in Hackney – one for women, at Gore Road, and for men, at Mare Street – was celebrated on 8 June 1980 at an open sessional reunion at the college attended by more than 400 participants. General and Mrs Brown were guests on this occasion and an ongoing appeal was made for funds to erect the cross on the college tower.

As principal, Harry's days were busy and fulfilling, organising the many innovations and special events, as well as the two sessions running concurrently and the need for him to get to know and mentor each cadet. From his earliest days of officership, encouragement had been his watchword, affirming, challenging and supporting those under his leadership. Harry encouraged the cadets to grow in their faith as they aspired to leadership in The Salvation Army.

How can I fail to grow
When Christ, my Saviour, dwells in me?
When he is so intent to show
My pathway and my destiny?

How can I fail to grow
When, past imagination's powers,
The Spirit gives my heart to know,
And feel, those blissful heavenly showers?

How can I fail to grow
When all I have to do is ask,
And grace, God's mighty grace, will flow
To make me equal to my task?

How can I fail to grow
When with the Lord I am an heir
To all the Father can bestow;
To love and strength beyond compare?

He also reminded them of the honour and privilege of their calling, referencing John chapter 15, verses 16 and 17: "You did not choose me, but I chose you and appointed you so that you might go and bear fruit – fruit that will last – and so that whatever you ask in my name the Father will give you. This is my command: Love each other."

Christ calls his followers to him by name:
"You did not choose me, I have chosen you."
Strong words of grace by which he made his claim
Within which lie his strength to see us through.

He calls you by your name! This fact implies
That in his plans he has for you a place;
A task to use the gift which in you lies,
Which only you can do, helped by his grace.

Because he calls you, you are in his care;
He will protect you – all your footsteps guide;
Will listen to each earnest, faltering prayer
And will your needs, your deepest needs, supply.

All you must do is worship Christ as Lord
And all the grace you need is his reward.

Another of Harry's responsibilities was oversighting the Thursday night holiness meetings held at Camberwell Citadel. For many years the cadets marching from the Training College to the citadel via a main road were a familiar site in Denmark Hill, with a few cadets appointed as traffic wardens and, in the winter months, lamp-carriers. As traffic density increased over the years, drivers' patience on the now very busy road understandably wore thin, and alternative routes were tried but eventually the march of witness had to be discontinued.

When Harry invited Commissioner Catherine Bramwell-Booth to speak to the cadets on the morning of a spiritual day, he offered to send an officer to transport her to the college by car. "That won't be necessary, Colonel," said the redoubtable Commissioner, "I have a gentleman who drives me around."

It was usual for the training principal to lead the meeting and introduce the special guest, who would speak for about

20 minutes, but that was not in Commissioner Catherine's plans. "I will conduct the entire meeting," she decreed, which she did, holding the absorbed attention of the entire assembly. Having been elected as 1977's best speaker by no less than the Guild of Toastmasters, this 94-year-old lady knew how to captivate her listeners while proclaiming her faith. "The commissioner was a total inspiration, and afterwards shared a midday meal at the college," Harry says.

Another guest speaker was Commissioner (Dr) Harry Williams, at that time the international secretary for planning and development at International Headquarters, instituted to respond to the growing needs of developing countries. Commissioner Williams, who had served as a specialist plastic surgeon for 30 years in India, was honoured with an OBE in 1970 and subsequently an Order of the Founder in 2005.

During its first three years the Planning and Development Department initiated almost 1000 overseas projects at a cost of £22 million. Commissioner Williams also invited Harry to be a guest speaker at a planning and development function.

Other inspiring speakers invited by Harry to the Training College included retired General Frederick Coutts, training principal for four years in the '50s when Harry was a sectional officer; Colonel Catherine Baird, who sparked Harry's poetic talent when he was a young cadet; and Ray Moore, the famous British broadcaster who compered The Salvation Army's *Banners and Bonnets* programme in the 1970s.

Open days held at the college attracted huge interest from Salvationists, dignitaries, local councillors and friends of The Salvation Army, with attendances of around 2000 people, raising funds for Training College projects including the lighted cross and a new electronic organ for the assembly hall.

Work at the college continued apace, and a 'teach-in' titled 'Evangelism through Visitation' was incorporated into the second-year programme, a cassette tape library was developed by the men's side officers, parents' days and open days continued to attract a large number of visitors and in 1980 the college's annual appeal raised a record £103,192.

Tuesday 27 January 1981 was a red-letter day – or, should it be said, evening – for the International Training College. General Brown had much pleasure in officially dedicating the 23-foot high floodlit cross on the tower, which became both a physical and spiritual landmark. A workman was reported to have said: "I shall never forget that I had a part in shedding the light of the cross over London."

A few days prior to the dedication, Harry had climbed a set of rarely used internal stairs leading to the top of the tower. "It was a delightful experience," he says, "and I could look out at the vista all around London. Interestingly, the tower was originally intended to be even higher but there was some thought by the architects that the extra height would impose too much pressure on the ground beneath."

Three years into his term at the Training College, Harry received a phone call from International Headquarters, stating, "General Brown wishes to see you." "I looked into my heart and thought, 'What have I done?', and it occurred to me that I was quite faultless," Harry says with a smile. "I phoned Win and said, 'I think we're going to move again.'"

After being ushered into the General's office and exchanging the usual pleasantries, Harry was astonished at the General's question: "Is there any good reason why you shouldn't go to Canada?" Harry was surprised because he had previously been told that his appointment at the Training College would be for five years, but after 33 years as officers he and Win looked forward to the challenge of serving The Salvation Army on another continent.

Reflecting on his time as principal at the Training College, Harry says, "It was a privilege; it was brilliant. I love the college's heritage and purpose; I love what it means in the hearts of thousands upon thousands of officers, not just in the UK but around the world. It was one of the most outstanding and fulfilling experiences of my officership."

In fitting synergy, Harry was succeeded as training principal by Colonel (later General) Bram Tillsley, whose previous appointment was as divisional commander of the Metro Toronto Division in Canada.

So it was that Harry and Win farewelled from the Training College, said au revoir to family and friends and journeyed to Canada, land of the maple leaf, to become chief secretary and league of mercy secretary in that vast country.

14

GOING ABROAD

Go into the world. Go everywhere and announce the message of God's good news to one and all.

~ MARK 16:15

After an eight-hour flight over the North Atlantic Ocean, Harry and Win arrived at Pearson Airport Toronto in August 1981 to an enthusiastic welcome from Commissioner John Waldron, Mrs Commissioner Helen Waldron and other members of the Canadian Territorial Headquarters staff.

Following their arrival, they were taken to their quarters and settled in to their lodgings on the 18th floor of a Toronto apartment building, with panoramic views across the city to Lake Ontario on one side and the airport on the other. They quickly adjusted to the Canadian way of life and soon felt at home.

The welcome meeting for Colonel Harry and Mrs Colonel Winifred Read, held at Jackson's Point Conference Centre, with prime frontage to Lake Simcoe, was one to be remembered. Led by Commissioner Waldron, who introduced Harry as a "parachutist, poet and preacher", the semi-formal gathering included warm words of welcome by representative speakers from the many facets of Salvation Army work in the territory.

At the conclusion of the meeting Harry and Win were greeted by crowds of well-wishers, including a retired officer with a broad Scottish accent. "Och aye," she said to Harry, "I came here expecting a Scotsman to be chief secretary and what did I get – a Yorkshireman!" Harry assured her he would do his best to live up to her expectations, despite his ancestry.

Harry found that his apartment building was within easy

commuting distance to Territorial Headquarters by car. For the first few weeks he was assigned a driver, who also worked at Headquarters, while Harry acclimatised himself to driving "on the other side of the road". Very soon he was confidently negotiating the city traffic in his own car during the daily commute.

In his usual proactive way, Harry had taken the initiative before leaving London of contacting Commissioner Waldron to request that a copy of The Salvation Army's Canadian Disposition of Forces be sent to him. Acquainting himself with the names of officer leaders in the territory for whom he would be directly responsible, he added them to his prayer list and wrote a personal letter to each of them, commenting on how much he was looking forward to meeting them and how readily he identified with the vision of the territory.

As he settled in to his new role as chief secretary, Harry soon found that working closely with Commissioner Waldron, an author, historian and inspiring speaker, was fruitful and fulfilling. "Commissioner Waldron, a US officer, was a superb, astute territorial commander, and I learned so much from him," Harry says.

Win's engaging and caring personality soon earned the deep affection of those she worked with and ministered to. During her time as league of mercy secretary, she gave leadership to 2600 members who visited more than a million people in hospitals and nursing homes each year. Interestingly, the work of The Salvation Army's league of mercy originated in Canada in 1892. "Win revelled in that opportunity and made very good friends," Harry says.

Soon after their arrival Harry and Win became grandparents again, with the birth of Margaret and Graham's daughter Lianne on 12 October. Less than a year later Lucy, their fourth grandchild, was born to John and Anne on 12 September 1982.

As second-in-command of The Salvation Army's operations in the Canada and Bermuda Territory, Harry had his work cut out. Stretching from the Atlantic to the Pacific and northward into the Arctic Ocean, at that time the territory was comprised of 16 divisions, almost 2000 corps officers and more than 400 corps and outposts, as well as many hospitals, wide-ranging correctional services and comprehensive social service programmes, many in partnership with the Canadian Government.

Harry was responsible for overseeing the Army's mission and operations, supported by the leaders of the various departments, including field, finance, social services, publishing, property, senior citizens, trade, training, correctional services, Red Shield services and information services – an extensive portfolio.

As well as corporate fundraising, there were also many Sally Ann thrift shops, as they were colloquially known, and the annual Christmas Kettle campaign, one of Canada's most recognisable charity events, urging donors to put money in the kettles and "keep the pot boiling".

Harry found the support of the assistant chief secretary, Lieut-Colonel Joseph Craig, and special service officer, Lieut-Colonel Gladys McGregor, invaluable. "There were numerous board meetings with influential members of the community, and meetings with officer leaders of the diverse social services operations of the Army," Harry says. "Joe and Gladys were brilliant sounding boards, and I was glad of their expertise and advice."

Serving on the Territorial Headquarters staff as field secretary was Harry's close friend Colonel Edward Read, a Canadian. Harry and Ed had much more in common than their surname. From their first meeting the two men had resonated, both being men of letters and empathetic, self-disciplined teachers of the Word. "Ed was a household name in his own country and his wife Doris was a lovely lady," Harry says. "Win and I really enjoyed their friendship."

They also enjoyed renewing their friendship with Captain Robert and Mrs Captain Gwenyth Redhead, who were serving in Canada at that time, Robert as director of the territory's Music Department and bandmaster of the Canadian Staff Band. Memories flowed from their collaboration more than 20 years earlier, when Harry was the writer/director of the commissioning pageants at the International Training College and Robert composed the music.

Before Harry's appointment to Canada, while he was principal of the International Training College, he had received an invitation to be a guest speaker at the Hong Kong version of the Keswick Convention, which he had agreed to at the time. He explained the situation to Commissioner Waldron, half hoping that he would demur, but the commissioner was quite keen and so the trip went ahead.

The Public Relations Department organised the details and, because Harry had a 12-hour wait during a stopover in San Francisco, they booked a hotel room so he could rest. However, when he got to Toronto Airport he was asked to show his visa allowing him to enter the United States.

"Canadians do not need visas for that and our PR folk had forgotten I'm a Brit," Harry says. "After much toing and froing the officials allowed me to travel under a restricted category of Travelling Without Visa. I had become a TWOV! My documents were taken from me and I was escorted to the aircraft. When we reached San Francisco I was told to sit in view of the check-in desk. After a while, I decided to risk an international incident by wandering around and having a meal before returning to my appointed seat."

When boarding time came, all the rigmarole of being handed over was repeated and when Harry reached Hong Kong – then a British colony – he became a free man again. The return journey was a repeat of the outgoing procedure. He was not impressed. In spite of the travel problems, Harry had a great time in Hong Kong. "They were kind, responsive people and I was glad to be there."

Because of the huge distances involved in visiting widely dispersed Salvation Army corps and institutions in Canada, Harry often had to travel by air. On one occasion he was scheduled to take a 'red-eye' flight to Anchorage, Alaska, changing planes in Winnipeg. On arrival there, he was advised by the Army's public relations man that they had to travel to another airport in order to take the connecting flight. Because of a traffic holdup they arrived late at the airport and Harry was told when he booked in that the plane had left the main building to taxi to the runway.

The PR officer must have been very persuasive, because the departing plane was returned to the boarding area. In full Salvation

Army uniform Harry walked up the steps, entered the plane and was shown to his seat, smiling and greeting the other passengers, who no doubt thought he was a VIP – which, of course, he was!

Harry and Win also journeyed on more than a few occasions to Bermuda which, although the island is situated more than 1000 miles from Canada and is in geographical proximity to the US, is under the jurisdiction of the Canadian Territory. Canadian officers began the work of The Salvation Army in Hamilton, Bermuda in the late 1880s. Because the islands were a British territory, the new venture came under the Army's Canadian command, an alliance that has continued to this day.

"It was always a lovely experience for Win and I to go to Bermuda and enjoy fellowship with the Bermudian Salvationists," Harry says. "Everyone in Bermuda knows everyone else. The corps were very effective and they shared well with each other. Bermuda is a proverbial tropical paradise, with pink sandy beaches and beautiful seascapes. It was a surprise to find there are no rivers or freshwater lakes and each house has tank water piped from the roof."

Another destination for Harry as chief secretary was the Quebec division, where French – decreed since 1974 to be the only official language in the province – is the mother tongue of seven million Québécois, although around 40 per cent are bilingual. The Salvation Army was well regarded in Quebec, with excellent corps and officers and a variety of services and programmes. With an interpreter on hand, Harry had no difficulty in communicating, and the Army's French connection was warm and welcoming.

After four years in office, General Arnold Brown retired at the end of 1981, and was booked to fly home to Canada. With Commissioner Waldron's permission, Harry organised an appropriate reception for the General and Mrs Jean Brown, only to get a message at the last minute that their plane had been delayed at London's Heathrow Airport because snow and ice had disrupted air travel. A few hours later a follow-up message said that flights had recommenced and the Browns would be arriving five or six hours later than originally planned.

A large reception room was immediately booked at Toronto's Pearson Airport where refreshments would be available and welcome speeches could be made. "When we arrived at the airport there was a large contingent of muscular rugby football players and their retinue of publicity men," Harry says. "One of the PR men asked me, 'What's The Salvation Army doing here?' I told him about General Brown, mentioning that he was one of the Army's best communicators, and the PR man asked if he could interview him." On his arrival General Brown was happy to talk to the interviewer and communicate the Army's message, before his welcome home in the reception room.

Harry and Win enjoyed taking part in Canada's Centennial Congress in June 1982, held in Winnipeg, the most central city of the vast territory. More than 6000 delegates, including visitors from 19 territories, joined in the celebrations. General Jarl Wahlström led the meetings, joined by retired Generals Arnold Brown and Clarence Wiseman. The congress events also included the commissioning of cadets trained in St John's, Newfoundland and Toronto, and the graduation of 57 nurses from Army's Winnipeg Grace Hospital.

A few months earlier, Harry and Win travelled to Vancouver to lead meetings celebrating the centenary. As part of the celebrations Harry unveiled a plaque to commemorate The Salvation Army's century of service in Canada. Topped by a Salvation Army crest, it reads: "This plaque unveiled by Colonel Harry Read, Chief Secretary for Canada and Bermuda, on Saturday, May 1, 1982 to commemorate The Salvation Army's Centennial 1882–1982. To God be the Glory." The plaque was unveiled at Hallelujah Point on the southeast side of world-renowned Stanley Park, with panoramic views of the Vancouver skyline. Hallelujah Point was so named because of early-day Salvationists holding open-air meetings in Stanley Park, their loud Hallelujahs being heard across the water to the city.

Soon after these historic events, after serving five years as territorial commander, Commissioner Waldron, and Mrs Commissioner Helen Waldron, president of women's organisations, retired. Harry had a huge regard for the commissioner, "an inspirational speaker, a tremendous organiser and a great writer", and Win had enjoyed working with Mrs Waldron. Commissioner Waldron's vision for the Catherine Booth Bible College (later Booth University College) left a lasting legacy, as did the many books he wrote during his retirement.

Stepping into Commissioner Waldron's shoes as territorial commander in September 1982 was Commissioner Arthur Pitcher, a Newfoundlander, described as "a holiness storyteller", who was also an author and accomplished public speaker.

"During our time in Canada we were very fond of Newfoundlanders – to us they were pure gold," Harry says. Newfoundlanders have certainly distinguished themselves in Salvation Army circles, with the Canadian province being the birthplace of two generals – Clarence Wiseman, elected in 1974, and Brian Peddle, elected in 2018 – as well as many other well-known Salvation Army leaders. "General Peddle and Commissioner Rosalie Peddle were young lieutenants when we were there," Harry says, "and they were very impressive."

The Salvation Army in Canada was thriving. As part of the territory's ministries of enrichment programme, a new Training College was built in St John's Newfoundland to accommodate the increasing numbers of cadets, and a library and heritage centre were added to the Training College in Toronto.

In September 1982, there was more positive publicity for the Army on the occasion of the opening celebrations of Roy Thomson Hall, a magnificent concert venue seating 2500, located in Toronto's entertainment district and home to the Toronto Symphony Orchestra. Harry and Win were among the huge crowd to attend the first Salvation Army festival, featuring the Canadian Staff Band, held in the brand-new hall.

Catherine Booth Bible College, the first-ever Salvation Army college for biblical studies and leadership training, and the Army's only degree-granting academic institution, opened its doors to students in September of that same year, including Colonel Ed Read's son Jim as a charter member. Harry presided over the opening day ceremonies in Winnipeg, and was an appointee to the board of trustees. The college was accredited by the government for the granting of three biblical and theological degrees in Canada: Bachelor of Arts, Advanced Bachelor of Arts and Bachelor of Theology.

Commissioner Pitcher was the commencement speaker, and also present were three earlier Canada and Bermuda territorial commanders: Generals Clarence Wiseman and Arnold Brown, and Commissioner John Waldron, whose far-sighted vision had provided the inspiration for the college from the outset.

Another centenary celebration was held in 1983, marking 100 years since the Army's correctional services began in an Ontario jail, assisting not only those who had broken the law but also victims of crime. The celebrations included exhibitions, a national conference and the opening of new correctional offices.

Commissioner Catherine Bramwell-Booth, the so-called 'grande dame' of The Salvation Army, celebrated her 100th birthday on 20 July 1983, and Harry and Win were among the thousands who sent her greetings. At her birthday celebration held in Regent Hall, London, led by General Jarl Wahlström, Commissioner Catherine testified: "Give to Jesus glory. That's what I'm doing tonight for his goodness throughout all my life."

During his time in Canada, Harry's poet mentor and shining example, Colonel Catherine Baird, was promoted to Glory. One of the many poems she wrote struck a deep chord in his heart, and in later years his poetic inspiration was to increase exponentially:

LINES TO A WRITER

When strong men lie divested of their power,
When youth is robbed of beauty's early flower,
When silver tones like echoes slowly die,
And useless riches all corroded lie –
Thy work shall teach the beauty of his will
When thine own heart is cold and thy lips still.
For unto thee, most honoured among men,

As to another one, he gave – a pen;
His hidden secrets hallowed in new Light,
To thee he whispers, then he bids thee: "Write!"

Winters in Canada were something to be remembered, with the lowest temperature Harry and Win endured being minus 34 degrees! "We had to wrap up warmly," he says, "because we had never experienced such cold before." He enjoyed the sight of hundreds of people – including some Territorial Headquarters staff – skating at lunchtime in Nathan Phillips Square, an urban plaza at the front of Toronto City Hall, and remembers the road and footpath snow ploughs that were swung into action after heavy snowfalls.

A visit to the famed Niagara Falls in the depths of winter was another unforgettable memory for Harry and Win. "The sky was blue, the sun was strong and it was bitterly cold. To our pleasure and surprise over the severe winter months the spray had built a wall of ice behind which the falls poured while the bushes and small trees around were covered in frozen spray. It was magical!"

They were also captivated by the stunning scenery in autumn – a season appropriately called 'the fall' in Canada – where the changing colours of the leaves form breathtaking vistas of red, orange and yellow. Toronto's prime destinations for autumn glory include High Park, Trinity Bellwoods Park and Scarborough Bluffs, where Harry and Win marvelled at the heavenly Father's handiwork.

While he was in Canada, memories of Harry's time as a wireless operator/signalman of the 3rd Parachute Brigade in World War II came flooding back when he was able to meet up with some of the paras from the 1st Canadian Parachute Battalion which had replaced one of the English regiments attached to the 3rd Parachute Brigade. "I got to know and work with the chaps from the Canadian battalion during the war, and was delighted to spend time with some of them again," he says.

Harry and Win were delighted when John, Anne and two-year-old Joanna visited them in Canada. As well as enjoying their time seeing the sights with Harry and Win, they also took the opportunity to visit some of the Canadian Territory's new corps plants, as they had been charged with opening a new corps in the north of England. Corps planting involves starting a Salvation Army outpost, opening a second congregation of an established corps, or pioneering a new corps, and the 'planting officers' were more than happy to share their experiences with John and Anne.

Margaret and Graham also visited Harry and Win with their two children, Mike, 3, and Lianne, who celebrated her first birthday while they were there. They spent a few days at the Army's Lake Skelton camp, staying in a lakeside cabin. When they arrived, two men brandishing shotguns warned them to be careful because a grizzly bear had been sighted in the area. Fortunately, the bear must have made tracks, and they holidayed in peace, including canoeing on the lake. They also took a cruise around Georgian Bay's 30,000 Bay Islands region, enjoying its rugged beauty.

Some time later, Commissioner Pitcher, who had previously been the territorial commander in USA South, organised for Harry and Win to spend a week's holiday in Florida as guests of the divisional commander, who arranged for them to lead Sunday meetings during their visit. While they were having a meal in the headquarters canteen, the divisional commander noticed that his public relations secretary was engaged in conversation with a visitor who happened to be the PR representative for Disneyworld. After Harry and Win were introduced, they were delighted to be invited by the PR man to be his guests at the world-famous theme park.

"So Win and I visited Orlando Disneyworld and the Epcot Theme Park Centre as guests of the management," Harry says. "What an experience! We loved every minute of it. We had never before been plunged into a world of so much imagination, ingenuity and technical skill."

With warm personal relationships always at the forefront of their ministry, Harry and Win often invited departmental heads to their quarters. "We had so many heads of department it was not possible to entertain them all at the same time," Harry says, "but we had a kind of roster and no one was excluded. They would come to our quarters, Win would prepare a meal and then we would discuss whatever was paramount before praying together." There was one such meeting in progress when the telephone rang.

Harry excused himself and took the call in another room, to be greeted by the Chief of the Staff, Commissioner Caughey Gauntlett, phoning from London on behalf of General Wahlström. "You are being appointed as the territorial commander of the Australia Eastern Territory with the rank of commissioner," he said. Harry returned to the meeting and continued with his usual aplomb, all the while bursting to tell Win the news. They would be taking up their appointment in June 1984.

After three memorable years Harry and Win were farewelled from Canada, with warm words of appreciation from Commissioner Pitcher, their many friends and Salvationists from around the far-flung territory.

Indicative of the lasting impression Harry made on the territory was this comment in a blog, written almost 40 years later, by Lieut-Colonel Fred Waters, at the time of writing secretary for business administration in Canada: "Commissioner Harry Read came into our lives just as we were heading off to college in 1981. He ... immediately won the people with his quick wit, calm spirit and evident spirituality."

Before taking up their new appointment, Harry and Win were delegates to a Salvation Army international leaders' conference held in Berlin, West Germany from 1-10 May 1984. Led by General Wahlström, the conference, titled 'Christ – Hope of the World', celebrated the unity of the global Salvation Army and its message of salvation in an increasingly divided world.

At that time the Berlin Wall brooded over the divided city, and Die Heilsarmee had been forbidden in the German Democratic Republic since World War II. Thanks to the Bishop of the Evangelical Church in East Berlin, the 116 delegates to the conference were given permission to cross the border and visit the church.

"Passing through Checkpoint Charlie, we had to have our documentation clear and without reproach," Harry says, "otherwise we wouldn't have been allowed in by the border guards, whose inspection even included checking underneath our vehicles with mirrors."

The conference delegates met for an uplifting meeting in the Reformed Church. After the benediction was pronounced there was an electrifying, God-glorifying time when Salvationist leaders from around the world spontaneously broke into song and the strains of 'O Boundless Salvation' – in many different languages – reverberated around the beautiful church.

Blessed and inspired, Harry and Win flew home to England after the conference, spending two weeks with family and friends before taking up their new appointment in Australia.

15

NEW HORIZONS

This land is God's land! Its rolling hills and plains!
This land is God's land, its city streets and lanes.
In hearts that love him truly, in lives that bring him praise:
For this land is God's land, Australia!

~ HOWARD DAVIES

Stunning panoramic views of Sydney Harbour, with its dozens of inlets, the iconic Opera House and Sydney Harbour Bridge, greeted Harry and Win as their plane prepared for touchdown at Kingsford Smith Airport in late May 1984. They had wisely avoided jetlag on the long journey by enjoying a two-day stopover in Singapore, staying with friends.

Although they had come from an early summer in England, the late-autumn weather in Sydney was as warm as their welcome by the chief secretary, Colonel Robert Bath, Mrs Colonel Mary Bath, and members of the Australia Eastern Territory Headquarters. At that time The Salvation Army in Australia was comprised of two territories – the Eastern Territory, based in Sydney, covering New South Wales and Queensland; and the Melbourne-based Southern Territory, encompassing the rest of Australia.

The Chief of the Staff, Commissioner Caughey Gauntlett, travelled from London to Sydney to conduct the public welcome and installation of Harry as territorial commander and Win as territorial director of women's organisations. Harry was delighted to meet the commissioner again, as they had worked together at the International Training College in the 1960s and interconnected in other appointments over the years.

Representative speakers at the welcome meeting, held in the

historic Sydney Congress Hall, included Commissioner Eva Burrows, at that time the territorial commander of the Australia Southern Territory, who declared she was there to "show the solidarity of The Salvation Army in Australia" and further cement the bond between the two territories. For Harry, the meeting was "an in-depth opportunity to share my prayers, my hopes and my vision for the territory".

Harry and Win's welcome meetings in Brisbane coincided with the annual congress and were attended by bumper crowds. During the afternoon praise meeting Harry was photographed while flourishing a boomerang that had been presented to him.

The evening salvation meeting brought much blessing, and the mercy seat was lined again and again with seekers, even after the meeting officially closed – so it continued. "Give to Jesus glory" the congregation sang in joyful exuberance before eventually leaving the auditorium.

Harry and Win soon felt quite at home in their quarters at suburban Rockdale. "The airport was little more than the proverbial stone's throw from our house," Harry says. "Oddly enough, the prevailing winds all seemed to be going the other way and we had no problems with the noise of planes, which we could see departing and landing."

Taking the helm at Territorial Headquarters, situated in the heart of Sydney's central business district, Harry lost no time in familiarising himself with the diverse operations of the Eastern Territory. His predecessor as territorial commander was Commissioner Howard Orsborn, son of General Albert Orsborn. "Howard Orsborn I knew very well," Harry says. "When I was a cadet he was my sectional officer at the Training College, and I had a great regard for him." Harry's enthusiasm knew no bounds as he worked with his 2-I-C, Colonel Robert Bath, to consolidate, continue and expand the ongoing mission of the territory.

Harry and Win quickly established a warm and convivial rapport with those under their command, Harry meeting with territorial headquarters staff, divisional commanders, corps officers, social services officers, cadets and retired officers, as well as members of the advisory board, while Win met with leaders of the various women's organisations.

Soon after their arrival in Australia they visited Colonel and Mrs George Carpenter, the son and daughter-in-law of the late General and Mrs George L. Carpenter. "The gracious and widely-experienced Colonel Carpenter's wise words to Win and I, as fledgling territorial commanders, were: 'You don't have to work harder, just hoist your sails higher to catch the wind of the Spirit.'" Colonel Carpenter's words became an indelible inspiration to Harry, articulated in a poem titled 'The Wind of the Spirit' he wrote some time later:

With sound of rushing wind the Spirit came,
His very nature full of mystery.
'Wind of the Spirit' his familiar name,
The cleansing, stirring wind of liberty.

Like trade winds he maintains his course with ease,
An evidence and means of massive power.
But oftentimes he comes a gentle breeze,
Caressing life and bloom on tree and flower.

"Great 'Wind of God', refresh our stagnant world,
Bring life to every mind and heart and soul,
Direct our ways as we, with sails unfurled,
Ourselves abandon to your strong control."

We need not strive a meagre goal to attain –
We higher hoist the sails, faith's goals to gain.

Harry and Win were also delighted to spend time with Commissioner Harry Warren and his charming wife Margrethe, who were enjoying an active retirement in Sydney. "They were very gracious," Harry says, "inviting us to their home on a number of occasions, and we had some lovely times together. Harry was writing his autobiography and I was his sounding board from time to time."

Visiting the Warrens involved a 30-minute trip across Sydney Harbour on the famous Manly ferry, an added pleasure.

The two Harrys may well have joked together about the Australian vocabulary. Harry and Win soon answered to being Salvos, i.e. Salvationists and – while never speaking Aussie themselves – soon got used to the laconic Australian way of shortening words by adding 'o' or 'ie'. For instance, muso, arvo, ambo (musician, afternoon, ambulance driver); and tradie, pollie, mozzie (tradesperson, politician, mosquito). Not exactly the Queen's English but quintessentially Australian!

Salvo had become a term of endearment and part of the Australian lexicon ever since the slogan for the annual Red Shield Appeal, 'Thank God for the Salvos', was introduced in 1969, with a national doorknock in May. Funds raised went towards family welfare assistance, women's refuges, homeless shelters, emergency and disaster relief, drug and alcohol rehabilitation, employment training, rural and outback chaplains, flying padres and prison chaplains.

From time to time Harry and Win visited Papua New Guinea, part of the Australia Eastern Territory since 1956 when Major and Mrs Keith Baker and Lieutenant Ian Cutmore pioneered the work of The Salvation Army in the island communities. Greeted by singing and dancing local Salvationists in their eye-catching, colourful costumes, Harry and Win were captivated by the people and the country, with its tropical heat, rainforests and rugged mountains and valleys.

"It was absolutely magnificent," Harry says, "like nothing we had ever seen before, a totally different culture, with whole villages becoming Salvationists." A commission encompassing the work in Papua New Guinea was established by Harry, to discuss and formulate a five-year plan for the further development of the Army in that country.

During October 1984, Lieut-Colonel John and Mrs Lieut-Colonel Gisèle Gowans visited Brisbane to lead 'Venture 84', a series of youth meetings attended by 1000 delegates from around Australia and the South Pacific region. Happy to see John and Gisèle again,

Harry introduced them to the crowd of young people at the initial meeting, and a series of vibrant and varied events followed under John Gowan's inimitable leadership.

The Army's emergency services were a focus of service in the territory, with emergency catering, chaplains, support workers and financial counsellors mobilised to give much-needed help when bushfires, floods, storm damage or drought ravaged local communities. "I used to marvel at the incredible courage of the firefighters and our folk who accompanied them and handed out food and refreshments," Harry says. "With courage like that in the national DNA it's no wonder Australians are so formidable on the sports fields."

Much loved in the community were the Salvos' Red Shield representatives whose service to troops during wartime was legendary. With their trademark 'Hop In!' signs complete with kangaroo pointing the way, Red Shield reps offered 'home comforts' to battle-weary soldiers in war-torn countries. The Red Shield Defence Services are still active today and Harry was more than pleased to meet representatives and commend them on their service.

"On three occasions I took part in the Anzac Day events in Sydney and realised just how much Australia had given to the world in flesh and blood," he says. "I also visited the Bomana War Cemetery in Port Moresby, Papua New Guinea and, as with every other military cemetery, my spirit felt the suffering, sacrifice and loss of life during wartime."

Harry and Win visited Broken Hill – also known as the Silver City, an inland mining community in the far west of Outback New South Wales, a vast, semi-arid area of more than 560,000 miles. The Salvation Army began work there in the late 1800s, ministering to the miners and townspeople, a work that continues today. They were also delighted to meet with indigenous First Nations Salvationists.

Captivated by the unique wildlife, including kangaroos, koalas and kookaburras, one of their outstanding memories when in the Outback was of an emu, with wings flapping, sprinting alongside the car they were travelling in at about 50 mph, until it was exhausted. "If it was trying to get away from us, all it had to do was to stand still or go in another direction," Harry says, still mystified at the emu's intention.

He also enjoyed taking to the skies with The Salvation Army's flying padres, Major Don and Mrs Major Eva Hill, on one of their visits to isolated homesteads in the Outback, a unique ministry that began in the Australia Eastern Territory in 1965.

The flying padres are hugely appreciated in the Outback. Their warm-hearted visits always bring much joy, and their Christian witness shines through in the thoughtfulness, kindness and care they so happily provide. They also conduct dedications, weddings and funerals.

Queensland's Centenary Congress, 'One Hundred Years – A Celebration', was held in Brisbane in September 1985, attended by more than 4000 Salvationists and friends. General and Mrs Jarl Wahlström, Harry and Win stood on the podium at the march past, with the General and Harry taking the salute.

It was a congress to be remembered, with Salvationists joyfully participating – bands, massed songsters, timbrel displays and pageantry, culminating with scores of seekers on Sunday evening and concluding with the full-throated singing of 'O Boundless Salvation'. A professionally narrated film of the congress is available on YouTube.

In April 1986, Harry travelled to London to take part in the High Council called to elect an international leader to succeed General Jarl Wahlström, who was due to retire on 8 July. A combined public farewell to the General and welcome to the members of the High Council was held at Westminster Central Hall. The high councillors were also invited to a reception by the UK Prime Minister, Margaret Thatcher.

Before he left Sydney, Harry wrote a song specifically for the High Council, with music by Major Howard Davies, and it was thoughtfully sung by the gathering of 46 High Council attendees, Salvation Army leaders from around the world.

Lord, God of Heaven's mighty host,
Whose powerful arm was Israel's boast,
Come, bless thine army here today,
Through this thine host, the power display.

Chorus:
We seek thy will, and thine alone;
We wage no warfare but thine own.
Thy mighty arm through us lay bare:
For thee, we fight, for thee we dare.

Our Saviour, Lord; our warrior King,
Whose triumphs through the ages ring;
Before thy cross we kneel in awe;
Behind thy cross we go to war.

O Spirit, come at Pentecost,
Whose gifts equip this mighty host.
Of love, so deep! Of wisdom's height!
Grant us the vict'ry through thy might.

The 11th High Council, convened by the Chief of the Staff, Commissioner Caughey Gauntlett, was held at Sunbury Court from 25 April to 2 May. Harry was surprised and honoured to be among the 13 nominees for General. Six nominees declined, leaving seven candidates: Commissioners Eva Burrows, Francy Cachelin, William Cairns, Andrew S. Miller, Harry Read, Mannam Samuel, and Colonel Wesley Harris.

With much prayer and reflection, Harry prepared a speech – as did all nominees – required to be submitted to the president of the Council, Commissioner Norman Marshall, beforehand. He was also required to answer the extensive general questionnaire for nominees, regarding both matters of administration and personal questions including past service, present health and any future contingencies.

Writing in *General of God's Army*, Colonel Henry Gariepy

commented that Harry was a strong candidate for the office of General. "Commissioner Harry Read … had a warm personality, was a proven spiritual leader and capable administrator, with solid international leadership experience. He was also well known for his poetry and verses of song."

After eight days of fellowship and deliberations, the members of the High Council came to a decision. When the results of the fourth ballot were counted, with the two remaining candidates being Commissioners Eva Burrows and Harry Read – who had previously received an equal number of votes – it was announced that Commissioner Eva Burrows had been elected the 13th General of The Salvation Army; incidentally, by the narrowest margin in Salvation Army history.

Two days later, Harry took the long plane journey back to Australia. "It was a night flight and I was sitting in a subdued kind of way, with mixed feelings, ruminating on the events of the High Council and its personal and spiritual value to me. I had a feeling of release – to have been there and for the vote to have been so close was a privilege and I wasn't at all thinking 'If only'. I had been honoured by the experience and there was peace and acceptance."

As the plane droned on through the night, in a moment of God-given inspiration Harry picked up a pen and paper and started writing, the words flowing effortlessly and spontaneously. From that moment his poetic inspiration took wings. "Under the guidance of God, my writing had a whole new impetus," Harry says, "and I was often led to write sonnets, being drawn to this lyrical form of poetry."

A further poetic inspiration came when son John visited Harry and Win in Sydney and during the course of conversation mentioned to Harry that he'd started a prayer journal. "I thought to myself 'What a splendid idea!'" Harry says. "My prayer life has always been very active, and when I finished my prayers I began to write poems in my journal. What a mystery prayer is! What a remarkable lifeline!" Harry became a prolific poet, losing count of the hundreds, if not thousands, of inspirational poems he has written during the many years since that time.

Soon after his return to Australia, Harry and Win travelled to Melbourne to conduct the farewell to General-Elect Eva Burrows, held in the huge auditorium of the Dallas Brooks Hall. The meeting was full of spectacle, and as he piloted the proceedings throughout the evening Harry referred to the pride of Australians in the election of Commissioner Burrows, and also read a poem he had especially written for the occasion.

One of the highlights for Harry and Win while they were in Australia was a reunion of members of the Humphries clan from Win's side of the family. Two of her predecessors of three generations ago had emigrated to Australia and lived in Bundaberg, Queensland. They became Salvationists and their descendants – quite a family of them – were held in high esteem in the community. When Harry and Win were scheduled to lead meetings at Bundaberg the family organised a reunion that was attended by more than 100 relatives.

And then there was the cricket. "On our first visit to Brisbane we were being driven by a PR man to a corps and he remarked that we were passing The Gabba [the Brisbane Cricket Ground, located in the suburb of Woolloongabba]," Harry says. "So many times as a boy I'd woken early to catch the cricket commentary from there and I asked the PR man to stop. The big Gabba gates were open and I walked in with no one asking who I was, and I just gazed wonderingly at this hallowed place. It set me up for the day!"

Harry was absolutely delighted that, as the territorial commander of the Eastern Territory, he was an honorary member of the Sydney Cricket Club and could have tickets for any game he chose to attend. Because of his busy schedule he managed to attend only two or three matches but "I liked the cricket and liked the fuss the club made of me," he says.

Under the heading of 'Poetry for the Present Age', one of Harry's poems was published in the Australian *War Cry* on 24 January 1987:

THE FAST BOWLER

The bowler broadly smiles, and then denies
That he the batsman would intimidate.
E'en though the ball at speed around him flies
It's not intended to decapitate!

No! Not at all! It keeps him on his toes;
Helps his reactions, sharpens up his skill;
"We're best of friends, as everybody knows;
Why would I want my good old mate to kill?"

Now life bowls bumpers to us all in turn;
The speeding ball just whizzes past our ears,
Our feelings churn within us, and we burn
As our imagination fans our fears.

Though circumstances can sometimes hostile be,
Within God's love is real security.

Having heard about Sydney's world-famous Bondi Beach, Harry and Win decided to go for a swim to test the waters. In the face of shark attacks at this and other beaches, huge shark nets had been installed, so they enjoyed their swim in the allocated area. "I wouldn't have minded so much being wounded in the war," Harry says, "but to be bitten by a mealy old shark would not be very much to my liking!"

When Harry's friend Colonel Dick Krommenhoek was asked to write a song for an upcoming European Congress in the Netherlands he contacted Harry in Australia asking him to write words to the music he had written. The title of the conference was 'Dare to be Different'. "Dick's music was dramatic and singable; for me, as a songwriter, the title was a gift and the words came quickly and easily," Harry says. Originally sung by songsters, 'Dare to be Different' was subsequently included in the 2015 Salvation Army song book.

I dare to live the life of faith,
The life of challenge God has planned:
Of holiness and victory,
For truth and righteousness to stand.

Chorus:
I dare to be different, I dare to believe.
I dare to be different, God's spirit receive;
I dare to be different, my life sacrificed;
I dare to be different by living like Christ.

I dare to ask the Spirit, come,
To match with power my heart's desire,
My life to cleanse and energise
With mighty Pentecostal fire.

I dare to want to live like Christ,
According to his will and way;
His love to know, compassion share,
And serve him boldly every day.

In a ground-breaking development, Harry, as the territorial commander of the Australia Eastern Territory, and Commissioner Donald Campbell of the Australia Southern Territory agreed in 1987 to establish a national secretariat, operating from Canberra, home to the Federal Government.

This meant that for the first time The Salvation Army would confer with the Australian Government as a single entity on issues including social welfare policies, housing, homelessness, and drug and alcohol rehabilitation. "We cut down on red tape and consolidated our work, speaking to government with one voice about spiritual, moral, ethical and social welfare issues," Harry says.

After three years in Australia, in a remarkable correlation of events, the circumstances in which Harry and Win received farewell orders bore a marked similarity to what they had experienced in Canada. "History can repeat itself," Harry says. Once again they were hosting a number of officers for a meal prepared by Win at their home, followed by an informal discussion and prayer about events in the territory, when the telephone rang.

Harry answered the call in another room, to find that it was General Eva, who after warmly greeting him broke the news that he and Win would be returning to England where he would become the British Commissioner. With perfect composure, he returned to the meeting and after their visitors left shared the news with Win.

At that time Harry's younger brother John – a high-ranking VIP in the financial world – and his wife Eugenie were visiting Sydney on business, staying at a five-star hotel. He had invited Harry and Win to share a meal with them at the hotel and when Harry told them of his appointment as British Commissioner, John, who no longer attended the Army, became quite emotional, extremely proud of his brother.

Following a fitting farewell at the crowded Sydney Town Hall, where they declared that their time in Australia was a highlight of their long years in officership, Harry and Win made their way to London to take up leadership of The Salvation Army in their home country.

DELIGHTED GRANDPARENTS

Harry and Win with grandchildren
Mike and Jo

On holiday with Margaret,
Graham, Mike and Lianne

Harry and Win with John and Anne's children, Lucy (left) and Jo

On Commissioner Harry's shoulders: the coming Army

Hallelujah Point, Stanley Park, Vancouver

Above: 1986 High Council nominees for General: *Top row:* Colonel Wesley Harris, Commissioners Andrew Miller, Harry Read; Front: Commissioners William Cairns, Eva Burrows, Mannam Samuel, Francy Cachelin

Right: Harry and Win on their way to Papua New Guinea

Below: Commissioners Eva Burrows and Harry Read meet Prime Minister Margaret Thatcher

Harry and Win enjoying early days of retirement

The first three editions of *Words of Life*, which Harry wrote for 10 years

Bible Study group at Winton Bournemouth Corps, with leaders Harry and Win

On holiday: passing Old Harry Rocks, Dorset

Heart Talk book launch at Winton with COs Paul and Julie Johnson, and Salvo Publishing's Dawn Volz

Enjoying a well-earned knickerbocker glory

Harry posts another poem to his Facebook page

Landing safely after a thrilling tandem skydive with Ryan Mancey

Harry with great-grandson Josh and granddaughters Lianne and Jo

Harry with Red Devils partner, Corporal Mike French

Jubilation after the jump,
with Sergeant Stacey Briggs

Skydiving with the British Parachute
Regiment's famed Red Devils

Above left: General Brian Peddle pins the Order of the Founder medal to Harry's uniform

Above right: General Peddle visits Harry in his home

Left: Harry presented with the Lègion d'honneur by French Ambassador Sylvie Bermann

Below: John and Margaret with Harry after the ceremony

16

FLYING THE FLAG

The greatest need is for evangelism. The best thing we can do for anyone is to bring that person into a good relationship with God.

~ HARRY READ

Jetting back to London in the spring of 1987, Harry and Win looked forward to returning to the UK and taking up their appointments – Harry as British Commissioner and Win as territorial president of women's ministries. It was a long and exhausting flight, and they were glad of a few days' respite before being reintroduced to comrades and friends at a grand welcome meeting in the Westminster Central Hall led by General Eva Burrows.

Soon after his arrival, Harry was featured in a BBC news broadcast, in which he succinctly declared the overriding mission of The Salvation Army: "The greatest need is for evangelism. The best thing we can do for anyone is to bring that person into a good relationship with God. We haven't done our best for someone when we've given them a meal or a bed, or counselled them about some marital problem, debt or whatever. We've done the very best for them when we've led them to God, through our Lord and Saviour, Jesus Christ."

Harry and Win enjoyed a convivial welcome at the Army's 101 Queen Victoria Street building in London, at that time shared by International Headquarters and the British Territory, each of which was provided with its own entrance. Having served for more than 30 years in the British Territory, they were no strangers to the headquarters officers. "I knew just about everybody," Harry says. "After being at the Training College for so many years, serving on the field, as the press officer and as a divisional commander, I had a wide range of friends."

Home for Harry and Win was a comfortable flat in a convenient location at Beckenham, nine miles from London and a few minutes' drive from Bromley, which became their home corps. Appropriate to his status as British Commissioner, Harry was assigned an assistant officer whose responsibilities included driving the official car, taking Harry to and from the office and other appointments. Harry occasionally went for a walk at lunchtime but usually had a communal meal in the large dining room before heading back to his office as soon as possible to continue his work.

As for family, after three long years during which – because they were unable to afford the airfares from Australia to London – they had not seen their grandchildren, it was an utter joy for Harry and Win to hug them again. Margaret and Graham's children, Mike, 8, and Lianne, 5, originally called Harry Poppa – later shortened to Pops (a name taken up by two succeeding generations of the Grayston family), while to John and Anne's children, Jo, 7, and Lucy, 4, he was Grandad (to the next generation of Reads he is Grandad Harry). Win was Grandma to all her grandchildren.

Margaret and Graham were stationed at Pokesdown Corps in Bournemouth, and John and Anne at Hull Icehouse Corps, and Harry and Win were delighted to lead meetings at their corps from time to time and catch up with the grandchildren.

Quickly taking the reins as British Commissioner, when Harry became aware that divisional commanders' councils had been organised to be held at Sunbury Court on a date soon after he took office, he immediately prepared a new agenda for the 40 divisional leaders who would be attending, setting out his vision for the territory.

At that time the British Commissioner was answerable to General Eva Burrows and the Chief of the Staff, Commissioner Ron Cox, and he enjoyed a good working relationship with them both. General Eva had established an advisory group of high-ranking officers and Harry was part of that cohort. She also requested him to be one of her standby consultants and he was sometimes called to her office for his comments and opinion.

"I was quite taken by the fact that the General not only asked for my advice but quite often took it," Harry says with a smile.

In his first territorial officers' councils, held at the Hayes Conference Centre in Swanwick, Derbyshire, Harry made an indelible impression on the hundreds of officers under his direction, telling them, "You have permission to fail." Years later, officers were to testify that those five words were liberating and life-changing. "Are you afraid of failure?" Harry asked them. "I am not giving you a mandate to close this, that and the other, but I am giving you a mandate to fail, *having tried*." He adds, "It was the message God had given me for our territory and people were very enthusiastic about it."

In October 1987, Harry and Win were among the hundreds of Salvationists and friends who attended the funeral of Commissioner Catherine Bramwell-Booth, CBE, OF, who was promoted to Glory at the grand old age of 104. On her 100th birthday she was quoted as saying she did not like the thought of death "because I am in love with life". On the other hand, she said, "If God had made this little short spell of life so beautiful, so full of wonders, what will it be like when he has prepared a place for us?"

Harry and Win made many visits to corps around the British Territory, and they travelled to Belfast, Northern Ireland's capital, to lead the meetings there on Remembrance Sunday, 8 November 1987. It was a Sunday they would never forget. After the holiness meeting they were enjoying lunch with Major John Brook-Smith, the divisional commander, and his wife Joan when the phone rang. Visibly shaken, John Brook-Smith told them that an IRA bomb had exploded near the Enniskillen town's war memorial during a Remembrance Sunday parade, held to commemorate British military war dead. Eleven people, including a police officer, were killed, and 64 were injured.

"John and I immediately decided to go to Enniskillen," Harry says, "and Wesley Pentland, the corps sergeant major from the Lurgan Corps, who I knew well, was only too pleased to take us. It was a rather harrowing hour and a half journey – seemingly every few minutes a helicopter would swoop low, approaching us for security purposes I was told."

Arriving at Enniskillen, they went straight to the Salvation Army hall, where a number of Salvationists had gathered to pray, while others were visiting families of the victims. Harry and John were taken to the bomb site and then to the hospitals where they visited the injured – including two Salvationists who were among the casualties – and counselled them and their families. John Brook-Smith was well-known for his sterling work on behalf of The Salvation Army in Northern Ireland, and was later honoured with the British Empire Medal.

A few hours later, they returned to the hall where people had been steadily gathering, having finished their visiting. "It was a very tired and solemn group," Harry says. "It was also time for me to thank them for their caring work and tell them how proud I was of them and how honoured I was to be part of their ministry to the town. After a season of prayer, we left to return to Belfast."

Harry recounted the story of a man named Gordon Wilson, who had been buried under rubble with his daughter Marie, 20, a nurse. They had been near enough to speak and hold hands but she later died in hospital. When Gordon Wilson was rescued, with great dignity he forgave the terrorists and with the same dignity, while expressing deep loss, faced the media. "I bear no ill will. I bear no grudge. I will pray for those men tonight and every night," were the unforgettable words of this saintly Christian man, touching hearts around the world.

During Harry's time as British Commissioner, *Marching as to War: The Story and Music of The Salvation Army*, a six-part half-hour television series produced by Anglia Television, brought the work of the Army into sharp focus. Presented by well-known British TV personality Roy Castle OBE, a committed Christian, the series caught the attention of the British public.

When the credits rolled, Lieut-Colonel Norman Bearcroft was listed as the musical director, Commissioner Harry Williams the series consultant and Captain Ray Begley the choreographer. The

International Staff Songsters also took a prominent part. "The programme was very popular and certainly celebrated the history of The Salvation Army and its continuing work and witness," Harry says.

Harry enjoyed renewing his long-time friendship with Norman Bearcroft, at that time national secretary for bands and songster brigades at IHQ. Many years ago, Norman's parents, Albert and Alma Bearcroft, had been appointed as newly-married lieutenants to South Bank, where Harry's parents were stalwart soldiers, and the two couples developed a lasting mutual affection.

When Harry was a side officer at the Training College, he accompanied cadets to visit retired officers in the Army's eventide home in the vicinity – "an inspiration to both the officers and the cadets," he says. Norman's complaint was that whenever he visited his mother, her main topic of conversation was that Harry Read had come to see her.

Harry and Win celebrated the British Congress, titled 'Make God's Army Grow', held from 1-3 July 1988 at Royal Albert Hall and led by General Burrows. There were scores of seekers at this event, which celebrated the Army's work in the UK, many aspects of which at this time were controlled by International Headquarters.

"They used to talk about the big five," Harry says, "the General, Chief of the Staff, finance secretary, social services secretary and the training principal, who controlled these operations in the British Territory while at the same time operating under the auspices of International Headquarters." Feeling frustrated by limitations on his leadership, where finance and fundraising, media contact, property matters and social services were controlled by International Headquarters, Harry was in no doubt that the territory needed to be self-sufficient.

The so-called 'British problem' was a historic dilemma that had been addressed through the years, beginning with General Wilfred Kitching in 1958 but, because of formidable constitutional, financial and logistical considerations, discussions had invariably reached a stalemate.

In September 1988, Harry and Win journeyed to Lake Arrowhead, a scenic mountain resort in the San Bernardino Mountains, California, to take part in a 10-day conference of international leaders, titled 'Towards 2000 – Vision and Task'.

Led by General Eva Burrows, the conference was attended by 115 Army leaders from 90 countries, with wide-ranging topics for discussion. Participants were reminded of William Booth's warning that The Salvation Army should beware of three dangers: stagnation, secularisation and self-satisfaction – issues still pertinent to the Army's progress more than a century later.

The agenda for the plenary sessions and discussion groups encompassed the Army's spiritual life and witness, as well as its leadership, structure, administration and management. Speaking from firsthand experience, with disarming frankness and candour, Harry addressed the issue of the seemingly intractable British problem, spelling out his frustration at the lack of autonomy of the territory. "My hands were tied," he says, "but I had the very strong conviction that this problem would eventually be solved."

Soon after returning to the UK, General Burrows appointed a commission to review the recommendations of the conference and discuss proposed solutions. Leaders in the planning process included Commissioner Ron Cox, Chief of the Staff; Commissioner Peter Hawkins, chancellor of the exchequer at IHQ; British Commissioner Harry Read; and Colonel John Larsson, who had been appointed assistant to the Chief of the Staff for UK administrative planning, with the specific task of addressing the so-called British problem.

On a lighter note, when Harry's older brother Wilf, then retired from his high-profile corporate position, saw an advertisement in *Salvationist* magazine for a senior finance role in the Army's Trade Department he applied for and landed the job.

"Wilf and I looked alike, sounded alike and had the same sense of humour," Harry says. Their resemblance was so strong that Wilf was amused when, making his way through the shop, he often heard Salvationist customers comment to each other, "Here's the commissioner coming, and he's not wearing uniform!"

Harry instigated gatherings that he termed 'Celebrations of Faith', evening meetings in various venues that followed consultations with corps officers in the afternoon. With contributions from a band and songster brigade (which Harry limited to one piece each), he gave the same address wherever he went, rallying the troops with a stirring message about growth, personal responsibility, commitment to evangelism, and the establishment of prayer groups. "I always had this drive for faith, witness and service. It was my message to them, and people were stirred to positive action to build their corps," he says.

From time to time Harry was invited by his good friend Commissioner Ed Read, then principal of the International College for Officers, to be a guest speaker at the college. Writing in his memoirs, *In the Hands of Another*, Ed Read said: "When Commissioner Harry Read visited us, the delegates were lifted to a level of excitement about their calling as officers that made me wish every officer in the world could spend time with us."

As for well-earned holidays, at one stage Harry and Win acquired a tent and thoroughly enjoyed camping out. With Harry's scouting experience, pitching a tent was no problem. Later on they bought a caravan that was sheltered in a farmer's shed near New Forest for most of the year. "Norman and Jill Bearcroft were expert caravanners – they took us under their wing and we enjoyed holidays together," Harry says.

On one of their furloughs, Harry and Win were invited by Margaret and Graham to accompany them and grandchildren Mike and Lianne on a visit to Normandy. More than 40 years after the war, they visited the place where Harry landed on D-Day and also the Ranville War Cemetery where three of his friends from the 6th Airborne Division were buried.

"It was a deeply, deeply moving experience," Harry says. "There was I with Win, Margaret, Graham and their two children, with John and Anne back in England with their two children. I had still so much ahead of me and my friends had only a gravestone with their names, regimental number and whatever text their families chose to honour their memory.

"For years I've contrasted the precision of the headstones in military cemeteries with the confusion and carnage of the battlefield. I've reflected further on the fact that soldiers on parade are uncommonly smart and in death their shattered bodies are gathered and they lie in their graves as though still on parade."

Harry's abiding friendship with Ray Moore, his high-profile broadcasting friend from the days when he was the Army's press officer, continued over many years. In the summer of 1987, when he rang Ray and his wife Alma, Harry was saddened to hear that Ray, a heavy smoker, had been diagnosed with incurable jaw cancer.

From that time on Harry became their spiritual counsellor and often visited them at their home in Greenwich. When Harry received a phone call from Alma to say that Ray had taken for the worse he visited him straight away.

"Ray was still cognisant," Harry says, "and I believe that in those moments I led him to the Lord. When he died he went to heaven – in my heart I am quite sure of that."

Ray died on 11 January 1989, just over a week after his 47th birthday, and Harry was honoured to be asked by Alma to conduct his funeral, to be held at All Saints Church Blackheath. Such was Ray Moore's fame that the BBC planned to feature a live television broadcast of his funeral. In consultation with Alma, Harry arranged for the International Staff Songsters and International Staff Band to take part in the service. The BBC representative wished to combine the Army's musical sections with other choirs and bands in massed items, but Harry was well aware that there was an Army regulation precluding that.

Conferring with the Chief of the Staff, Commissioner Ron Cox, Harry explained the situation, to be told that because of the regulation it would not be possible. With all the diplomacy he could muster, Harry replied that the cost of saying the Army could not cooperate with the BBC would be far higher than the consequences of working with them.

"May I say that if you give me permission and it doesn't work the original regulation can be restored," Harry said. The go-ahead was given and the camaraderie of the combined choirs and bands paved the way for Army musical protocols to eventually be updated, ushering in a new era of friendship and opportunity for witness.

Later that year, in October 1989, Eric Ball, another long-time friend of Harry's, was promoted to Glory at the age of 85 years. Eric's wife Olive passed away in July 1988, and after he was no longer able to look after himself due to failing health, a little group who knew and loved him, including Harry, considered the options for Eric. They were delighted when the Winton Bournemouth bandmaster Stan Randell and his wife Mary offered to look after him in their home.

Eric was a soldier of the nearby Poole Corps and, as his health became more concerning, he discussed his funeral with Norman Bearcroft, his close friend. Norman suggested that Harry, also Eric's longstanding friend, former corps officer at Hanwell and now British Commissioner, should lead the service, to which Eric readily agreed.

When some time later Eric was promoted to Glory, Harry led the service at Poole Corps, with the corps officer also taking part. Following the funeral, a festival celebrating the incomparable life and legacy of Eric Ball was held in the evening at the much larger Boscombe Citadel, during which Harry read a poem he had written for the occasion.

At certain times, death comes to us as friend;
With gentleness he stands inside the room;
He tells that burdens now are at an end
And, in the name of Jesus, whispers, "Come".

Earth's open door is closed without a sound
While life as mortals know it is no more,
And opened is the door to heaven's ground
Where reigns the King whom heavenly hosts adore.

Where all is peace and glory's purest light –
The air, song-filled with joy and praise,
Where trophies of God's grace and love and might
Pay tribute to God's kindness and God's ways.

Our brother, Eric Ball, is with his Lord;
A faithful, loving child of God's great grace;
He bows before the Christ whom he adored –
Looks up – and reads his welcome in Christ's face.

The Salvation Army's sixth International Congress, 'With Christ into the Future', was held in London from 29 June to 8 July 1990, attended by 20,000 Salvationists, with 3570 registered delegates from the Army's 50 territories and commands. The 10 days were packed with meetings and also three-day seminars covering the multi-faceted work of the worldwide Salvation Army, including ministry, church growth, personal evangelism, Bible study, youth work, music, drama and Army theology, to name a few. Assisted by Colonel Ed Read, Harry was the session leader of a Church Growth seminar, following an International Strategy for Growth Conference in London in 1989, which was attended by 92 delegates from around the world.

He vividly remembers an International Congress Sunday meeting at the Royal Albert Hall when, after giving an inspiring sermon, General Burrows called on him to lead the prayer meeting. Tenderly and fervently he encouraged members of the huge congregation to search their hearts, and there were hundreds of seekers.

A few months later, on 1 November 1990, after two years of protracted deliberations piloted by Colonel John Larsson, the inauguration of The Salvation Army's United Kingdom with the Republic of Ireland Territory was celebrated at Westminster Central Hall. Fittingly, the newly-promoted Commissioner John and Mrs Commissioner Freda Larsson were welcomed as leaders of the new territory.

Commissioner Larsson paid tribute to his mentor: "Commissioner Harry Read brought a wonderful spirit of optimism to the

UK Salvationists through his leadership as British Commissioner. Mine was the privilege to build on that. And mine was the privilege of bringing together the various 'armies' in the UK in a way that had never been possible before."

These events coincided with the culmination of Harry and Win's 42 years of service as Salvation Army officers as they entered retirement. General Eva Burrows conducted their retirement meeting at the packed Regent Hall, at which many of their family members were present. Glowing tributes were paid and they received prolonged applause from the congregation.

Among the many legacies of their time as British leaders was the innovation of a National Council for Salvationism, a group of officers and Salvationists which met six times a year to offer advice to leadership; a layman's Brengle Institute at Sunbury Court; and an adherents' recruitment programme. Major and Mrs John Dangerfield were appointed to lead the newly-established Department of Church Growth, and a seminar programme was inaugurated for both officers and soldiers.

"I knew it was to be a demanding last appointment," Harry says, "and it was, but it was more than challenging, it was exhilarating, with fulfilment to match my dreams. What a privilege! Others must be left to evaluate my ministry and that of my darling wife, but though we faced the immense difficulties inherent in an increasingly godless society and a decreasing Church – and Army – our service was blessed by God."

17

WORDS OF LIFE

For whatever was written in earlier times was written for our instruction, so that through perseverance and the encouragement of the Scriptures we might have hope.

~ ROMANS 15:4

After such an eventful and dedicated life spanning four decades of service as leaders in The Salvation Army, it could be expected that Harry and Win were looking forward to a well-earned rest, but that was far from the case. With retirement came fresh opportunities for ministry.

For the first few years Harry and Win continued living in the same quarters at Beckenham and continued their service at Bromley Corps. Win had a preference for being a hospital chaplain and when the local Council of Churches minister/chaplain retired Win was canvassed for the job, accepted it gladly, and was in her element.

Harry was asked by the Bromley corps officer, Major (later General) Shaw Clifton, to lead an evening Bible study, but as there was already a similar event being held in the evening, Harry felt that a morning time slot would be more suitable. Very soon afterwards a large group gathered each week at 10 am on Thursday mornings to meet in upstairs premises at Bromley Temple and enjoy a cup of tea before settling down to study the Word under Harry's inspirational leadership. Someone in the fellowship remarked, "This is like an upper room, isn't it?" and from that time on the Bible study became known as the Upper Room.

Another opportunity was in the offing for Harry when he was contacted about a well-paid position with a leading Church Growth organisation. He had worked with them previously as a guest lecturer, for which The Salvation Army was paid the substantial sum in those days of £150 per lecture, plus expenses. However, before the Church Growth appointment could be finalised, the Chief of the Staff, Commissioner Bramwell Tillsley, asked Harry to consider writing *Words of Life*, the Army's international daily devotional book.

Distributed three times a year (January-April, May-August and September-December) by British publishing house Hodder & Stoughton (now an imprint of Hachette) on behalf of International Headquarters, *Words of Life* contains day-by-day readings and commentary, providing readers with food for thought, praise and prayer, points to ponder and cross-references for further study.

The Soldier's Armoury, forerunner to *Words of Life*, was launched in 1955 by Literary Secretary Colonel Catherine Baird, Harry's mentor, and published twice a year before being retitled *Words of Life* in 1989. Over the years, a succession of gifted writers, including Harry's good friend Major Ken Lawson, who wrote and edited *The Soldier's Armoury* from 1985 to 1988, provided inspiration to many thousands of Salvationists and other readers around the world. With daily messages, *Words of Life*, now a four-monthly publication, ran to around 120 pages and was priced at £1.99.

"Since I'd rather work for the Army than anyone else, I accepted the responsibility for *Words of Life* and the rest is history," Harry says. "I loved doing it. It still allowed Win and I time to do a lot of specialling and continue to lead the Bible study."

Taking over from Major David Dalziel for the January-April 1992 edition, Harry's first message read: "January is a month of new beginnings. So many of us take stock at the beginning of the month and decide that there are some things we are going to start, or old things we are going to do better. It is a new beginning for me since this is my first volume of *Words of Life*. I confess to being challenged and excited at the prospect of sharing an adventure in faith and prayer with you."

During his always busy life, even in retirement, Harry readily accepted the exacting task of writing a daily devotional for 365 days a year. Deciding at the outset that his messages would be positive and creative, inspiration flowed freely and his many years of biblical scholarship came to the fore. He decided to alternate each month between an Old and New Testament character, his first edition featuring Abraham, Matthew, Isaiah and Jesus.

Having been provided with an Apple Mac computer by the International Headquarters Literary Department, an added challenge was to familiarise himself with a Mac after previously using an IBM personal computer. When Harry was British Commissioner some of his peers at headquarters were content to delegate learning the skills of the digital age to their secretarial staff. However, with encouragement from his family and close attention to *Computers for Dummies,* Harry soon progressed from typewriter to computer keyboard. "I readily embraced the technology," Harry says. "The more I used the computer the more I liked it." It was the transition from PC to Mac that was the new challenge here.

The prelude to 'All Things New', a poem he later wrote, thanks God for a life of challenge, discovery and inspiration:

O Lord, you have great secrets to unfold,
Great principles to highlight and commend,
New heights for me to scale and views behold,
New concepts to discern and comprehend.

New truths on which to pray and meditate,
New plans whereby your will might best be done,
New skills your strategy to activate,
New grace to finish work in grace begun.

New openness on my part to receive,
New zeal and energy for this great task,
New faith that on your word I might believe,
New boldness as for more of you I ask.

All that I have become, O Lord, refine,
That I might incarnate your plan divine.

In late August 1991 Harry and Win travelled to Australia to lead Sydney-wide congress meetings, after being invited by Commissioner Robert Bath, who had been the chief secretary of the Australia Eastern Territory during Harry's time as territorial commander. The jam-packed days included a rally titled 'Let's Celebrate', during which octogenarian Commissioner Harry Warren sang 'I'm Nearly 83 Lads', accompanying himself on his concertina, which brought the house down. Harry and Win were delighted to renew their friendship with the Warrens and their many Australian friends.

The Sunday morning holiness meeting, the march past, afternoon gospel rally and evening salvation meeting were joyous and well-attended, with more than one hundred people making decisions during the congress events. Harry and Win's itinerary included three sessions of officers' councils and a luncheon meeting with retired officers. They also visited Melbourne, caught up with some long-time friends, spoke at a Brengle Institute faculty and led Sunday meetings at local corps during the two weeks they were there.

That overseas visit was the first of many Harry and Win made in retirement. Opportunities to speak at officers' councils and the occasional congress in other territories followed, and Harry was in high demand.

"Once I'd starting writing *Words of Life*, it seemed that I was on a speakers' circuit, and Win and I were invited to do various congresses and seminars, mainly in the United States. It was something I very much enjoyed and was a real blessing."

Retirement was not a word in Harry's vocabulary. A life of leisure? Not for him. "I love work," he says, "I like the cricket but I love work." While writing *Words of Life* and leading the Bible study at Bromley, he was requested to become the interim principal of the International College for Officers because the principal, Commissioner Ian Cutmore, had been hospitalised and needed a lengthy recovery time.

So Harry and Win spent a number of weeks at The Cedars,

34 Sydenham Hill, South London, home to the International College for Officers – originally called the International Staff College – since 1954. The college curriculum included worship, prayer and spiritual growth, doctrine and leadership development. While enjoying their studies, the delegates were buoyed not only by Harry's leadership but also the unique camaraderie they shared with fellow Salvation Army officers from around the world.

"Major Lyn Pearce was the assistant principal and had set up the curriculum," Harry says. "We got to know and appreciate Lyn during our time in Australia and her expert help was indispensable. I became principal for a full session but I couldn't have done it without Lyn's expert help. I was there at 8 am preparing to lead the majority of the day's activities – it was challenging and enjoyable."

Farewelling from Bromley and their many friends in 1996, Harry and Win made the move to Bournemouth and, after settling into a flat close to the seaside, thoroughly enjoyed life in this beautiful coastal town in the south of England. As John and Anne were at that time stationed at the Winton Bournemouth Corps, and Harry and Win's good friends Norman and Jill Bearcroft soldiered there in retirement, a warm welcome was assured.

A consummate musician and composer, Norman was invited by the bandmaster, Stan Randell, to join the percussion section of Winton band, while as the self-confessed "worst second horn player in The Salvation Army" Harry had no such musical ambitions.

Harry and Win quickly became treasured members of the corps and were soon leading a weekday Bible study at Winton, attended by 50 to 60 people. The community hall in which the study was held was a little distance from the supply of song books in the main hall and it occurred to Harry that he could save the chore of collecting and returning the books if he wrote an opening and closing song relating to the subject they were studying.

"This I did for a number of years, hence the high number of songs I've written," Harry says. "If I write a poem or song in connection with a subject I've been working on, the inspiration comes naturally and quite quickly. If, however, I'm writing to order I have to get into the subject first. That takes time but once I'm at home with the subject the rest follows without much difficulty." All this while in his fourth year of continuing to write *Words of Life*.

While Harry and Win were drawn to the seaside, he wasn't enamoured with sitting idly on the sand for any length of time so he wrote to the Bournemouth Borough Council requesting a long-term hire of one of the beach huts that sat alongside the sandy environs of Bournemouth beaches. The short answer was that there were none available.

However, when one of the elderly ladies at the corps who had rented a beach hut passed away Harry again wrote to the council and tactfully commented: "Presumably there is now a beach hut available and I'm sure that my departed friend from The Salvation Army would have been delighted to know that we could take over her annual licence." This time the short answer was yes.

Harry and Win spent many happy times at the beach hut that was situated on Alum Chine beach, west of Bournemouth, a quiet area facing Poole Bay, with a wide expanse of sand away from the bustle of Bournemouth Pier. Sometimes while Win enjoyed the sand and the sun, Harry would sit in the beach hut, pen in hand and notebook on knee, working on another edition of *Words of Life* while intermittently gazing at the blue sky and rolling waves.

There is a silence where God can be found,
A quietness which is a source of grace,
A love-filled solitude which has no bound,
Accessible at any time and place.

It is that centre wherein God is known
And love, sublimest love, holds total sway,
We enter it as we approach his throne
And share its mystery when best we pray.

He draws us to himself with tenderness,
He longs that of himself we should be part,
Our hopes he fills with yearning's gentle stress,
That we might share the beat of his own heart.

Within that most creative solitude
Our deepest inward being is renewed.

Family time was important to Harry and Win and they caught up with John and Anne and Margaret and Graham whenever they could. Margaret and Graham had a caravan and also sometimes went to France on holiday, leaving from Poole and passing the white chalk cliffs of Old Harry Rocks, a famous landmark comprised of three chalk formations on the southernmost tip of the Jurassic Coast in Dorset.

According to one of the stories about how the landmark came to be known as Old Harry Rocks, they were named after the devil, sometimes known as Old Harry, who legend has it once fell asleep on the rocks. Harry and Win chuckled when Margaret sent them a postcard depicting Old Harry Rocks. Margaret's message on the back was: "Ahhh, but does he roll?"

During Harry and Win's retirement, 1995 became a watershed year for married women Salvation Army officers when, under the direction of General Paul Rader, their status changed and they were granted rank in their own right. Rather than Mrs Commissioner Harry Read, Win finally became Commissioner Winifred Read. "Win was a wonderful Salvation Army officer," Harry says. "She lived equality, never serving in a subservient manner. She was a marvellous role model for not only women officers but all women."

With the 50th anniversary of D-Day approaching in 1995, Harry was asked by Colonel Henry Gariepy to write an article for the US *War Cry* about his service with the 3rd Parachute Brigade in World War II and, of course, he agreed. He wrote the article in three instalments and included a poem in each. Harry and Henry, kindred spirits and men of letters, had been long-time friends. Henry was for many years the national editor-in-chief and literary secretary in the US, and in 2007 was awarded the Order of the Founder for his exceptional service.

Harry was also listed as an advisory consultant in Henry's epic publication, *Mobilized for God: The History of The Salvation Army*

Volume Eight 1977-1994, published in 2000. In addition, Harry wrote a recommendation, featured on the back cover of the book: "This is history recorded in fine style. It informs the mind, inspires the heart, and makes exciting, fascinating reading."

As the new millennium dawned on 1 January 2000, Harry had his own heartfelt message for the Army he loved: "I believe our name, The Salvation Army, is an inspired designation, born not of human wisdom but of the Holy Spirit. I believe also in the timelessness of the divine qualities that built our Army. I am proud of all that our relatively small Army has achieved. God has used our greatly gifted people to best advantage and we who are ordinary confess that he has used our ordinariness wonderfully well. Each one of us has an important part to play in the salvation war."

Harry and Win keenly followed the proceedings of The Salvation Army's International Millennium Congress led by their old friend General John Gowans from 28 June to 2 July 2000. Held at the World Congress Centre in Atlanta, US, there were more than 20,000 registrants from around the world, making it the largest ever gathering of Salvationists.

Few would ever forget the inspiring message of General Gowans as, using a three-legged stool as an illustration, he declared, "The Salvation Army is supposed to have three legs." Tapping the first leg, he said, "It was invented by God to save souls," the second leg, "to grow saints" and the third leg, "and to serve suffering humanity. When we do those three things we're as solid as the Rock of Gibraltar."

The theme of the Millennium Congress, 'The Army Next – Carrying the Flame into the Future', resonated around the Army world. And after serving as Salvation Army officers for 52 years, 10 of those in dynamic retirement, the flame still burned brightly for Harry and Win.

18

NO HEART MORE TENDER

The true glory of human love is that it binds us with God who is the source of all love.

~ HARRY READ

Revelling in their busy retirement, and enjoying occasional holidays, visits from family and the warm comradeship of the Winton Corps, Harry and Win were fulfilled and content as the years went by. But clouds were beginning to appear on the horizon.

In 2002 Harry began to notice that Win's memory was faltering, a condition which became more concerning over the next few months. As time progressed, her confusion, difficulty with everyday tasks and changes in mood increased and she became increasingly dependent on Harry for assistance.

Caring and concerned, he made arrangements with their doctor to have Win undergo a test to determine her problem. She was resistant but eventually went with Harry to meet with a nurse and undergo a preliminary series of questions, the results of which were inconclusive. "Well, that was a waste of time, wasn't it?" she said to Harry. Unconvinced, he arranged a follow-up test, which resulted in her being referred to Bournemouth Hospital for further investigations, after which she was unequivocally told, "Mrs Read, you have Alzheimer's."

Determined to stave off the steady progression of this cruel condition, Win's diligence with crosswords, Sudoku, code words and anything that would keep her brain active had to be seen to be believed, Harry says. "Win was blessed with a gentle loving nature but at the same time she was incredibly strong. She also possessed a powerful gift of prayer, and the engaging transparency and simplicity of a saint. We had the perfect marriage largely due to Win's love, patience and wisdom."

As caring for Win became more pressing, Harry was reluctantly compelled to discontinue writing *Words of Life*. During his long tenure from 1992 to 2002, he had contributed almost 3500 daily messages and countless affirmations of faith and words of wisdom.

At an appreciation lunch held in his honour at International Headquarters, the Chief of the Staff, Commissioner John Larsson, said: "The name of Harry Read has always been associated with creativity, but after almost 10 years of continuous creativity on *Words of Life*, the time has come for him to hand over the torch. On behalf of the thousands of readers of *Words of Life*, we thank you for all you have done."

Judith Longman, editorial director of the Religious Division of Hodder & Stoughton, publishers of *Words of Life*, also paid tribute to Harry, remarking on his impressive achievement of – not surprisingly – never missing a deadline. Harry was presented with a Bible and two books on behalf of the publishers.

In his response, Harry had a heartfelt word of thanks for special guest and long-time friend Colonel Will Clark, a former literary secretary, for his input and assistance over the years. Will had lived across the road from Harry in their childhood years, and they had farewelled from the Grangetown Corps to the International Training College together way back in 1947. Summing up, Harry said, "*Words of Life* has been one of the most beautiful things that has ever happened to me, in a lifetime of beautiful things."

As Win's symptoms of Alzheimer's inexorably progressed, she became more and more reliant on Harry as her source of comfort and strength. He had set up the third bedroom of their flat as a study, where he worked on his desktop computer, but on realising Win needed his company he eventually spent the "vast sum" of £800 to buy a laptop so he could sit with her in the living room as he worked during the day. It was heartbreaking for him to experience the slow degeneration of the love of his life, and though his faith never wavered, this was the prayer of his heart:

O Lord, I lift my heart to you for you to fill;
These days with their demands have left me drained.
I would again be centred in your will,
My heart replete with you, by love sustained.

There is no other source of life for me,
No other hand which can true peace bestow,
No other voice with words of liberty,
No other mind which can my own mind know.

No other God my heart to overwhelm,
No other goal to be my life's great aim,
No other guide to take life's unsure helm,
No other Lord, who knows me by my name.

Enfold me, Lord, make me both strong and sure
Life's race to run – and evermore endure.

As time went by and Win became lost without Harry's constant presence, he felt it necessary to give up leading the Winton Corps Bible study after many years of meaningful fellowship with so many regular attendees who were blessed by his leadership and biblical knowledge. Harry's care of Win was love personified.

When they went on holiday to Majorca – not knowing it would be their last together – with Margaret and Graham, Win was no longer able to walk very far and Harry told her he had ordered a wheelchair. "Who's the wheelchair for?" she asked. When Harry said it was for her, she said, "I'm not sitting in a wheelchair." Quickly stepping in, Graham said, "I'll tell you what – I'll get in the wheelchair and you can push me and when you think it's time for me to get out I'll push you." As Graham could do no wrong in Win's eyes, she readily agreed and their holiday proceeded. It was a happy time but filled with emotion as they realised that Win was fast becoming increasingly frail.

Forever etched on Harry's memory is the night of 4 June 2007. Just after midnight while he was in the bathroom getting ready for bed he heard an unfamiliar noise and hurried into the bedroom where he saw that Win had collapsed on the floor of their en suite. He tried to lift her but she was in terrible pain. Harry immediately called for an ambulance and the paramedics arrived within minutes, transporting Win to Bournemouth Hospital, while Harry followed in his car.

Arriving at the emergency department, he found that Win had been admitted without delay and was being assessed by the doctors. "In spite of the exceptional care she was given, Win never regained consciousness. While in the hospital she had a cardiac arrest from which they resuscitated her but she faded quickly from that point and went to be with the Lord at about 3.30 am."

Harry spent precious time with Win – indescribable moments of overwhelming love and grief – before returning home and at 5 am writing an email to their many friends to tell them of Win's passing and the sadness that enveloped him. "My life with Win, and Win's life with me, was of God's ordering. Her death, and my life without her, are still part of his providence – his constant care," he wrote. A few days earlier Harry and Win had celebrated their 57th wedding anniversary.

I am bereaved, but I am not bereft.
The grieving consequence of death I feel
But God is loving and his hands are deft;
And tender is his touch my heart to heal.

My heavenly Father writes his love in me;
Unswervingly he claims me as his own.
His arms enfold me unconditionally
To grant the peace that comes from him alone.

My soulmate I have lost just for a time –
The day of reunion soon will dawn
But I am not bereft! God's love is mine,
Providing proof that death's sting is withdrawn.

God's promises forever he will keep;
Their benefits forever I will reap.

With achingly poignant timing, later that same day, on 5 June, Harry and Win's great-grandchild, Elise, was born to Lianne and Paul, who had beforehand asked Harry to write a song to be sung at Elise's dedication. The first words of the song read: "It was a heavenly kind of day – a day of glorious dawn."

When those words were sung at Elise's dedication service, Harry asked himself, "Was that really 'a heavenly kind of day'; was it not rather my darkest day?" That question was dispelled in a poem he later wrote: "My sadness was eclipsed by heaven's joy; my pain transcended knowing she was healed... Win was called home. Dare I resent that call? That day was not my darkest, after all."

Win's crowded remembrance service, held at the Winton Corps, was led by the Chief of the Staff, Commissioner John Larsson. It was a time of love, joyful memories, thanksgiving for Win's life, and sadness at her passing, keeping in mind that, in Harry's words, "She shares the life of Christ in highest glory, the fullness of her destiny to find." Prior to the Thanksgiving Service, the Winton band played as Win's casket arrived at the chapel of the Bournemouth Crematorium for a moving Service of Committal, attended by family and a few close friends.

After being bereaved of Win, Harry's sorrowing soul took gossamer wings. With deep emotion he wrote many poems, sharing them with three men in the corps who were also grieving after the recent loss of their loved one. They told Harry how reassuring and meaningful his words were, and he began to think perhaps others could be similarly helped and blessed.

In the meantime, he continued his busy and fruitful days, spending time in prayer and devotions, and expressing his unwavering faith in an ever-increasing number of poems. "I had become a compulsive writer of verse," he says. With his pastoral spirit, he visited friends from the Bible study group and those whose links with the corps had become tenuous over time, including some who were ageing and lacked transport to the Sunday meetings.

After Win died, Harry never went down to the sea again except when his family visited and suggested an outing to the beach.

"Because it brought back so many memories of Win, if I wanted to be lonely – which I never did – I would go down to the sea," Harry says pensively. He offered their beach hut to a Salvationist couple from the Sheffield area who often visited Bournemouth, and they were delighted to take over the lease.

Less than a year after Win's passing, a phone call late in the evening of 9 May 2008 broke the silence in Harry's flat. And it was shocking, totally unexpected news. Margaret's husband Graham, hale and hearty and in seemingly great health, had passed away. He and Margaret were visiting a retired officer couple and had enjoyed a meal before relaxing and chatting together when Graham was suddenly taken ill, and within minutes was literally fighting for his life. An ambulance was called and the paramedics did everything they could but he was pronounced deceased when Margaret and their friends arrived at the hospital.

Graham died from heart failure. Unbeknown to him and Margaret, he had a genetic heart condition and that evening, when an artery became blocked without warning, he suffered a fatal heart attack. In the majority of cases, those with this condition often have symptoms of extreme breathlessness or angina, but Graham was among the 20 per cent who have no sign of any problem.

Margaret, Harry, family members, a few close friends and representative bandsmen farewelled Graham at a chapel service led by John. Graham had enjoyed great fellowship while playing trombone in the Cannock Corps band during the eight years he and Margaret served as corps officers there. As the hearse drove past the Cannock Citadel, a large crowd of comrades and friends stood silently, with heads bowed, in tribute to him.

Then followed a thanksgiving service at the citadel, led by John and Anne, celebrating Graham's life of 56 years. His sudden loss was keenly felt. Graham was kind, compassionate and gracious, with a great sense of humour that he often used to good effect while leading Sunday meetings. Harry remembers that Graham, a fellow Yorkshireman, had a set of drink coasters with the droll message, "Tha can allus tell a Yorkshireman but tha canna tell 'im much."

Margaret had asked the band to play Sir Edward Elgar's 'Nimrod', a profoundly beautiful and reflective musical masterpiece and one of Graham's favourites. During the service there was a time of tribute when Anne invited those in the large congregation to take part. One by one, many people stood and told of how Graham had touched their lives and how his encouragement had strengthened their faith. For Margaret, he was not only a wonderful husband and father but also her best friend.

"Graham was a perfect son-in-law," Harry says. "He was a great chap in so many ways. He used to do the pubs with the *War Cry*, and in their little town there was an ideal place in the main street where he would sell – or give away – copies of *War Cry* and *Young Soldier* magazines. Graham knew everybody and was in his element. He was a fine man."

Those heartfelt sentiments were echoed in a poem Harry wrote for Graham's thanksgiving service:

From earth to heaven – from here to there
Is but a human heartbeat long.
From faith and hope to answered prayer –
By just one heartbeat heaven is won.

And, like a soldier, Graham marched in
To angel song and trumpet call,
That life eternal might begin
With Christ, the King, his all-in-all.

His passport was his heart of love,
A passport bearing Christ's own seal,
Graham's guarantee of life above
Where all God's promises are real.

And what of us left here to mourn?
Do we not glimpse heaven's glorious light?
Perceive the glad perpetual dawn
That glows through sorrow's darkest night?

Are we not meant to follow Graham,
Our hearts drawn by the risen Lord,
Then with the saints in glory claim
Eternal life as our reward?

A few weeks before Graham's sudden passing, he and Margaret had been appointed to Divisional Headquarters at Exeter, after serving at Cannock Corps for so many years. Unable to take up that appointment, Margaret became divisional family officer in the Southern Division and lived in Southampton, not far from Harry in Bournemouth and her son Mike and his family in Portsmouth. Always close to her Dad, Margaret says during this time Harry became her rock, and being able to frequently visit him became a lifeline to her.

As Harry pondered his experiences of bereavement and talked with others, he felt a strong conviction that the poems he had written during his darkest days could be a source of reassurance and blessing to those who were also mourning the loss of a loved one. He contacted the Literary Department at International Headquarters, submitting the manuscript he had prepared and asking, "Do we have a book here?" "You most certainly have," came the answer, and the book, titled *No Heart More Tender*, was presented to the Literary Board for appraisal and approval.

Produced by Salvation Books, the book publishing imprint of International Headquarters, and blessing readers around the world, *No Heart More Tender* is still available today from Salvationist Publishing and Supplies.

As time went by, Harry reached a point where, in his words, "young drivers in their fast cars made it quite clear that this old man [Harry was 85] shouldn't be on the road any more". He talked to John and Margaret, who were in total agreement, so he and Margaret went house-hunting and eventually he moved to a lovely flat in Dean Park Grange, Bournemouth, close to shops and transport, including a bus that took him right to the door of the Winton Salvation Army hall.

Harry was asked to contribute to *Hallmarks of The Salvation Army*, by Colonel Henry Gariepy and Major Stephen Court, published to honour General Eva Burrows on her 80th birthday in 2009. He wrote a definitive chapter on Salvationism, "an unusual phenomenon: a spiritual force with a life-changing potential".

"Salvationism is an engine-room kind of word, for within its robust, energy-exuding frame pulsates the heart of the Army. All the big words of Christianity find their place within this engine room word: unconditional love, sacrifice, forgiveness, grace, acceptance, faith, hope, intercession and burden-bearing..."

SALVATIONISM
(A gift from God's heart)

From my own heart I make this gift to you—
A gift of unconditional love and grace.
If to my heart-to-heart gift you are true
You will more often seek me face to face.

Your fellowship with one another will
Reflect my love and joy—my focus on the Christ:
Your mutual care and prayer will help fulfil
The plans for which my Son was sacrificed.

Go, in my name, claim your community:
The sad, the weak and each aspiring soul,
Let Pentecost be your authority—
Tell them and show them, I can make them whole.

Salvationism is a word of power
And your Commission for this crucial hour.

Reflecting on the momentous events of his octogenarian years, sometimes with an aching heart, Harry's implicit faith and resolute spirit carried him through, as he relied on the promise in Isaiah chapter 30, verse 15, "In quietness and confidence shall be your strength."

19

A GOOD READ

When I was a lad, thrilled by the great poets and marvelling at their work, I never dreamed of the ministry awaiting me through poetry.

~ HARRY READ

Twenty-three years after his official retirement as a Salvation Army officer, Commissioner Harry Read's 65 years of ministry were about to take a new direction, in a way he could never have previously imagined.

First things first. Harry was delighted to be father of the bride once again when Margaret married Major Norman Ord on 18 February 2012. Although Harry and Win and Norman's parents, Commissioners John and Lydie Ord, had served together and knew each other well, Margaret and Norman had never met until they connected on Facebook.

They were married at Sunbury Court by Norman's cousin, Major Hélène Carey. Norman was at that time the principal of the William Booth College (generally known as the International Training College until the year 2000 when the name was changed), where his father John was a cadet in the same session as Harry and Win so many years ago, while Norman's mother Lydie followed a year or two later.

So it was that Facebook first brought the newlyweds together. The introduction of the internet in the 1990s sparked an online revolution, and the so-called information superhighway eventually became the preferred medium of everyday global communication, not least Google and Facebook. While Harry utilised his computer for word processing and emails, participating in social media was not on his agenda.

Little did he know that when Margaret set up a Facebook page on his behalf back in 2007 it was eventually to be the catalyst for a new era of spiritual encouragement, with Harry's poetic gifts becoming an instantaneous inspiration for a worldwide audience. However, despite Margaret's encouragement, for the first few years Harry was less than enthusiastic about sharing on social media, and the following message appeared on his Facebook page on 24 April 2010:

"☺ Hello all friends – I'm putting this on for my Dad. Just to say, he's not got the hang of Facebook, so isn't ignoring any of you, just doesn't know which button to press! He may come off Facebook at some time in the near future – but wants you all to know, no offence is (ever) intended – and he's glad to have so many friends." Similar messages ensued in the following months.

As time went on, little changed and Harry began to wonder whether he should close his Facebook account. "At that moment," he says, "it seemed as though the Lord was rebuking me for my lack of vision. 'Maybe, just maybe,' he seemed to be saying to me, 'you might have a contribution to make.'" Inspired by that spiritual prompting, Harry switched on his computer, intent on meeting the challenge.

While confessing to his followers that the processes tended to bewilder him, in an effort to prove that – in his words – at the age of 88 "an old dog can learn new tricks", Harry prayed and persevered until his keyboard resounded to a new rhythm of grace. So it was that, at age 88, with prayer poems as his focus, Facebook became his platform and Facebook friends his congregation.

At this time, he also began to realise the potential of the internet to proclaim the gospel worldwide: "We cannot leave this ever-expanding field to commerce and other interest groups," he says. "Salvationism is not limited to yesterday's methods, although many of those methods are valid and fruitful. Our faith and vision affirm that the wonderful opportunities of the internet are among the fields ripe unto harvest."

Harry's first Facebook poem appeared on 10 July 2012:

O Lord, I cannot of myself achieve
Those objectives that faith and love require.
Nor by my native energy believe
That I can match with deeds my heart's desire.
I need the gift of all-sufficient grace –
I need the grace that goes to any length –
Which gives me victory where my path may trace
The grace that turns my weakness into strength.
Thank you, Lord.

Harry's earnest prayer was answered in spades. His fledgling Facebook page grew wings and today – more than 800 poems later – his almost 5000 Facebook friends from around the globe follow his beautiful encouragement to "read these poems with the eyes of your heart".

Representative comments from his Facebook followers speak eloquently of the deep blessings his inspirational poems bring:

"Your poetry is tender, touching, real and reassuring …"
"Holy, precious, uplifting, encouraging words …"
"A delightful tonic …"
"Thank you for soul food …"
"As eloquent as the angels …"
"Moving, poignant and appropriate …"
"I can barely see the page for tears – these words are truly God-inspired …"
"Your words are reaching deep down into my soul …"
"Each line jumps off the page with power …"
"You never fail to inspire …"

In 2013, on the other side of the world, in Melbourne, Australia, the Australia Southern Territory Literary Council, under the leadership of Captain Mal Davies, deliberated about publishing Harry's poems in book form, under the banner of Salvo Publishing. Council members were unanimous in their agreement and the decision was made to contact Commissioner Read with the proposal.

When the first contact was made in April, Harry was delighted, sending a number of poems during the following week. Wasting no time, the Literary Department made regular communication and within weeks the book of poems was well on its way. *Heart Talk: The give and take of communion with God* was the apt title Harry chose, and the process of collating the poems, editing and proofreading continued apace.

The Literary Department's graphic designer had drafted a front cover featuring a beautiful white rose, but Harry had more eye-catching ideas. During his time as territorial commander of the Australia Eastern Territory, he became captivated by the majesty of the Blue Mountains, a vast region of mountaintops, sandstone cliffs and forested valleys, 40 miles west of Sydney. The Blue Mountains' most famous site, a trio of rocky pinnacles called the Three Sisters, was featured on the book's striking cover.

On an introductory page of *Heart Talk*, Harry commented: "The Blue Mountains were regarded as an impenetrable barrier to expansion inland by the early settlers in Sydney. Thirty-three years after settlement, three men, Blaxland, Wentworth and Lawson, attempted to conquer the barrier by following the tops of the ridges – and succeeded.

"As Christians, we choose the high road of sacrifice, endurance, prayer and faith, following in the steps of Christ, our untiring guide, constant companion and ultimate goal."

Heart Talk contains more than 150 poems, under the headings of God the Father, Jesus the Son, the Holy Spirit, plus Gifts of Spirituality, Prayer, Faith and Love. Also included are poems for special occasions, including Christmas, Easter, dedications, weddings, bereavements, and Remembrance Day.

One of the faith-affirming poems under the heading 'The Gift of Love' references 1 Thessalonians 1:4: "For we know, brothers and sisters loved by God, that he has chosen you, because our gospel came to you not simply with words but also with power, with the Holy Spirit and deep conviction".

ASSURANCE

Chosen, claimed and equipped
How can I fall when you have bid me stand,
When you have chosen for my life success?
When even in disaster you have planned
My greatest good, my highest blessedness?

How can I lose my way when you are near,
My life's companion, my unerring guide?
You give me courage when my heart feels fear;
Behind your hand I confidently hide.

I am your child! And this, Lord, by your choice;
And by your choice my sinful heart is whole.
Then will my soul with all the saints give voice
That you are God! And you my life control.

My heart will sing your praise forever more,
And will forever your great name adore.

Another poem, under the heading of 'The Gift of Faith', rings particularly true in troubled times. "Miracles of faith are waiting to happen," says the prelude to the poem:

THE CHALLENGE OF TODAY

These times of challenge call for miracles.
The cynic's view of life and death abounds.
While greed and selfishness make obstacles,
And clever arguments the young confound.

If there's a time for faith, that time is now.
Our enemies have grown like giants tall.
Too many at the shrines of evil bow
And Jesus chides us that our faith is small.

We lack real power because of unbelief.
It slips our minds that faith is God's planned way

Whereby his erring children find relief
And we God's enemies and ours can slay.

Faith is our need and faith God's offered gift,
Which faith, said Christ, can make a mountain shift.

The foreword to *Heart Talk* by General Paul A. Rader and Commissioner Kay F. Rader speaks for itself: "These poems are remarkable for their honesty and human quality. They emit the fragrance of a holy life with eyes fixed on Jesus and the things above." General Rader also remarks on "the elegance and emotive force of the language, the disciplined symmetry and beauty of expression ... the spiritual wisdom and understanding tempered by time and the rigours and rewards of Harry's faith journey".

Heart Talk came highly recommended, with glowing comments by Salvation Army leaders, including the following:

"A collection of poems that reflect the journey of the soul and give expression of a real humanity through a deep personal faith. Plunge in, breathe deep as these writings nurture, comfort and uplift your human experience with our creator God." ~ Commissioner (now General) Brian Peddle.

"Commissioner Harry Read is living proof that generations, decades apart, can adjust and connect with one another, and that adaptability to change is no respecter of persons. Cyberspace has become his platform, Facebook his pulpit and poetry his medium." ~ Commissioner Joe Noland.

Five months after the book was first proposed, *Heart Talk* was launched at the Winton Bournemouth Corps on Sunday 8 September 2013 at a meeting conducted by the corps officers, Majors Paul and Julie Johnson. Soon after the meeting's end, the number of books available for the launch was sold out, with Harry kept busy signing copies for his many comrades and friends. Further demand meant that a reprint was necessary and *Heart Talk* is also now available as an ebook.

"Because almost all of my poems have been born in my daily prayers or meeting preparation, they're particularly precious to me," Harry says. "Poetry, music, painting and other creative activities can only be produced as the result of a gift. God's people believe such gifts are God-given. Of course we have to nurture the gift and hone our skills – possession of the gift carries also the responsibility to use it."

Inspirational poems, of course, are not Harry's only God-given gift, and over the years he has written the lyrics of many songs in consultation with a number of well-known Salvation Army composers including John Larsson, Robert Redhead, Dick Krommenhoek, Howard Davies, Andrew Blyth and Mark Bearcroft. His best-known songs – 'God's Soldier', 'Become Aware of Him', 'We Are an Army' and 'I Dare to be Different' – have become long-lasting classics, sung with gusto in Salvation Army meetings.

"I enjoy writing songs," he says, "it is much the same as writing poems. Very often I write verses which can also be sung and every now and again one of my Facebook friends suggests that the poem I have posted that day can also be sung to a certain well-known hymn tune.

"If confession is good for the soul," he continues, "I get extra pleasure when a song goes up on the screen in Salvation Army meetings, because I look for the technical bits: the metre, the rhyming pattern, the careful choice of words, and the progression in the verse. As succeeding verses come up I'm looking for the development of the song – the strength of the last line of each verse and, particularly, the strength of the last couple of lines of the last verse. All the time I'm singing heartily and appreciatively."

Harry was one of the contributors to *Tsunami of the Spirit: Come Roll Over Me*, a collection of writings honouring General Paul Rader on his 80th birthday in 2014. Edited by Commissioner Joe Noland and Major Stephen Court, the title was based on an inspirational quote from General Rader: "Pray that a Spirit-inspired movement of prayer … will bring a mighty tidal wave of salvation blessing … a tsunami of the Spirit, cleansing, refreshing, and renewing us for mission."

"God wraps some of his gifts up in the oddest of parcels," began

Harry's chapter. He evocatively likened the emergence of The Salvation Army from its chrysalis of humble beginnings into a vibrant worldwide expression of Christianity, to a caterpillar becoming a beautiful butterfly, a pearl created in a drab grey oyster shell, or a dull brown bulb producing a magnificent flower.

"As part of Christ's body on earth, we are privileged to do his work and do so with a contagious joy. That's Salvationism: that's the kind of Army we are," he wrote, concluding with the words of his song 'We Are an Army Mobilised by God'.

Arguably, none of Harry's songs has been more widely sung than 'God's Soldier', with music by John Larsson, written for the International Training College cadets' commissioning pageant in 1962, an anthem much loved by Salvationists in the more than 50 years since.

Although Harry was unable to attend the events of 'Boundless', The Salvation Army's 150th anniversary celebrations held at the O2 Arena in south-east London from 1-5 July 2015, he would have thrilled to the full-throated singing of 'God's Soldier' by the huge congregation of Salvationists who packed the arena for Session Three on Founders' Day 2 July, and Session Five on Friday evening 3 July, where the song was the triumphant finale.

'God's Soldier' was the only song to be sung twice during the celebrations, its spirited message celebrating future challenges. "We're going to fill the world with glory… We're going to smile and not frown… We're going to sing the Gospel story… We're going to turn the world upside down!" The singing of the crowd raised the roof as thousands of Salvationists joyfully affirmed their faith.

Harry's songs were also a feature of his son John's retirement meeting, held in July 2016, after 37 years as a Salvation Army officer. Harry was very proud of John, who had been awarded a BA from the Open University, an MA in Theology from King's College London and a PhD from Manchester University for his research into the life and work of Catherine Booth. Major (Dr) John Read's last appointment was as ecumenical officer for the United Kingdom with the Republic of Ireland Territory, and chair of the territory's moral and social issues council.

Anne, who planned the retirement meeting, included the song 'Become Aware of Him', which had special significance for John as Harry had written it with him in mind, and the meeting concluded with another of Harry's songs, 'I Dare to be Different'.

A few months later, in October 2016, Harry was honoured by the French Government for his service in World War II. The words of the first verse of 'God's Soldier' were particularly pertinent on this occasion:

God's soldier marches as to war,
A soldier on an alien shore,
A soldier true, a soldier who
Will keep the highest aims in view.

Having served under two flags – Britain's Union Jack in World War II, and the yellow, red and blue Salvation Army flag for the rest of his life – Harry Read is indeed God's soldier. His two allegiances came together in fitting fusion when, proudly wearing his Salvation Army uniform, he was honoured with France's highest distinction, the Légion d'honneur, in recognition of his role as a British paratrooper during World War II.

The ceremony was held in the impressive surroundings of what had originally been the ballroom of the French Ambassador's residence in Kensington Palace Gardens, London. Ambassador Sylvie Bermann presented 92-year-old veteran Harry Read with the Chevalier award by order of the Légion d'honneur, the highest French order of merit, both military and civil.

Harry takes up the story: "The French Ambassador – a lady – with her entourage entered, taking her place on the podium. With gentle, pleasing skill she welcomed us and launched into a generous and articulate expression of her country's indebtedness to those who, after some of Europe's darkest years, had been prepared to give their lives to liberate France.

"With a couple of much be-medalled French officers the ambassador stepped from the podium and approached the

13 nonagenarians, plus one centenarian, to award the medal. One of the attending officers read out a biographical synopsis of the recipients of the medal in turn, who, with much pleasure and dignity, rose to have the medal pinned on. Even the two wheelchair-bound men managed to stand. Again, the personal greeting from the ambassador was warm and generous."

Established in 1802 by Napoleon Bonaparte, the award has been retained by all later French Governments and regimes and, following the 70th anniversary of D-Day in 2014, then French President François Hollande pledged to honour all British veterans who had served in his country during World War II.

The Légion d'honneur is represented by a red ribbon, an oak and laurel wreath and a five-armed medal with the head of Marianne, the national symbol of France, on one side and two tricolour flags with the motto 'Honneur et Patrie' (Honour and Fatherland) on the other. As the ambassador pinned the Knight Medal of the Légion d'honneur on Harry's uniform, he was almost overcome with emotion as he recalled the events of D-Day, 72 years before, and the sacrifice of so many of his countrymen.

Reflecting on receiving the award and his time with the 6th Airborne Division, Harry says: "The French Government was at its generous best when it decided to honour, with this highly prestigious medal, those who took part in the liberation of France.

"My feelings are of pride but it's a pride tempered with an awareness of the enormous cost of the thousands of lives needed to achieve victory. How cruel war is! How important too that, being a survivor, my life should be lived to serve God and to serve the community! This also I've been honoured to do."

Harry's Légion d'honneur award aroused the interest of the media, and he was in demand for interviews after the ceremony, including one for the British Forces Radio Service. There was also an invitation from the Mayor of Bournemouth to appear with him at the local launch of the Royal British Legion Poppy Appeal. After being interviewed by the mayor, Harry was given special-guest status, enjoying tea and cakes with the mayor and his wife.

A few weeks later, Neil Barber, a military historian, writer and researcher especially interested in Harry's 3rd Parachute Brigade, visited him at his home for an in-depth interview, arriving just before 10 am and departing at 3 pm. Harry was kept busy during the interview and, ever the congenial host, provided soup and a dessert for lunch. "It was a good time," Harry says. "I'd prepared for his coming by typing out some headings and grouping memories around them and it was interesting to see how his findings and mine dovetailed."

During their conversation Neil informed him that in 2017 there would be an officially organised celebration in Normandy on 6 June, the 73rd anniversary of D-Day. He thought Harry would appreciate going and mentioned that he could easily arrange for him to be part of the group. "From the moment he said that the thought went through my mind, 'I'd love to do a parachute jump!'" Harry says.

Harry's appetite for a further visit to Normandy was certainly whetted by his conversation with Neil. Having revisited the area for the first time since World War II with Win, Margaret, Graham and their two children in 1978, he was more than tempted.

After thinking further about it and discussing it with his family, Harry rather reluctantly decided against taking the journey. But his lingering bouts of nostalgia meant that was not the end of the story. A year later his interest was rekindled when John suggested a father-and-son trip to France in the summer of 2018, and this led to the thought that they could visit Normandy and attend the series of remembrance services for D-Day.

On enquiring about a prospective visit, Harry was told that a World War II veteran, plus his spouse and/or carer, was entitled to an all-expenses-paid five-day visit to Normandy in conjunction with the D-Day celebrations. After talking to John the next day, Harry wasted no time in contacting the organisers and, with great anticipation, made a booking.

20

COME FLY WITH ME

Once you have tasted the taste of the sky, you will forever look up.

~ LEONARDO DA VINCI

As the time neared for Harry's upcoming trip to Normandy, vivid memories of his D-Day experiences and the subsequent three months on the battlefields of Normandy came flooding back and he looked forward to the visit with a mix of poignancy and high excitement.

In his preparations, he realised that the new red beret he had ordered to replace his original one that was beyond redemption, was too pristine to be worn properly. "Traditionally," he says, "a new beret needs to be left out in the rain, thrown around the barracks room, used as a duster and then cleaned up. Only after such tribulations can it be worn with honour." So he placed his beret out in the rain and hoped for more rain the next day.

As his two medals were badly tarnished, he checked online for advice on cleaning them and, after dismissing the more complicated methods, chanced on the comments of a veteran who suggested using a simple pencil rubber, which he found brought them back to their shining best. He could now rest in the knowledge that his para regalia was all present and correct.

Harry and John left on Monday 4 June and, rather than flying to Normandy, travelled by coach and channel ferry on a tour initially originated by veterans of the 6th Airborne Division and sponsored by the Parachute Regiment.

The journey started in London and they were able to link in at Portsmouth before taking the six-hour ferry trip as it crossed the busy English Channel. After their arrival at Caen they took a two-hour coach trip to Cabourg, where Harry and John stayed the night. Although it had been a long and demanding day for Harry, when his head hit the pillow he looked forward with pleasure to the upcoming D-Day celebrations.

At the welcome dinner the next day, somewhat to his surprise Harry was invited to sit next to Lieutenant General Sir John Gordon Lorimer, Colonel Commandant of the Parachute Regiment. He was a gracious man and Harry enjoyed not only the honour of speaking with him but also the pleasure of his company.

In the course of their conversation Harry mentioned that he would have very much enjoyed the challenge of taking part in a tandem parachute jump to commemorate D-Day and regretted that no such arrangements had been planned for that year. "The General could have been forgiven for thinking that a 94-year-old of indeterminate health contemplating a sky dive from 20,000 feet was indulging in a flight of imagination," Harry says, "but he was very receptive."

General Lorimer pointed out that the next year would mark the 75th anniversary of D-Day and tandem jumps were being arranged for that occasion. Joining the conversation, one of the General's colleagues, Major Adam Jowett, who was involved in the organisation of D-Day celebrations for 2019, promised Harry he would be first on the list to take part in a tandem jump. All he needed to do was to stay well and get a doctor's certificate verifying his health. Harry could hardly wait to tell John the news, and as they continued their travels there was much discussion about their future plans.

"The trip to Normandy was a great time – sombre at times – especially the ceremony held on Wednesday at the Ranville Airborne Cemetery where I stood at the graves of my friends," Harry says. "Such sad, tender moments. The passage of the years only emphasises their enormous loss. So many men died – so many of them like me who had just left their teenage years for the battle."

A poem he wrote, 'Where Comrades Rest', movingly expresses his feelings:

Weep not for those who lie in this cold earth,
They rest like heroes in their hallowed grave,
As men upon whom destiny from birth
Decreed they would a world from bondage save.

Shed then no tears, for they no tears have shed,
As they a mighty enemy o'ercame;
These men chose noble sacrifice instead
Of meek submission to a tyrant's claim.

And yet, our hearts are moved, and tears we weep
As we consider all these men have lost;
Their previous hopes and plans by guns made cheap,
By war's red hands into oblivion tossed.

How great their sacrifice; how great our debt;
We need our tears, lest we that debt forget.

During Harry and John's visit the weather for much of the time was quite cold and it was frequently raining. Thursday, the day before the contingent left for the return trip to England, was the exception and the sun shone brightly. John hired a car and they visited the places where Harry had served in World War II, including Le Mesnil, the area he and his para mates had so bravely defended for many weeks. Obviously much had changed – time had healed the scars of war and the battlefields that had seen so much loss of life were serene, green and peaceful.

"As we travelled the various stages of the route," Harry says, "and I shared with John the memories of the strategy and battles, the losses and victories as we pursued the enemy as far as the River Seine, so much more flooded back into my memory."

Following his visit, Harry wrote a letter thanking the organisers for the excellence of their program and to his surprise they replied appreciatively, at the same time asking for his suggestions for the next year. It was later indicated that at the 75th Anniversary Celebrations of D-Day in Normandy he would be jumping with the Red Devils, the official parachute display team of the British Army and the Parachute Regiment. As professional skydivers, the Red Devils perform more than 350 tandem parachute descents and 60 public displays each year in the UK and internationally.

Harry was to discover that, after exiting the aircraft at 10,000-14,000 feet, depending on the weather and air traffic clearance, a tandem skydive involves a freefall of around 30 seconds, reaching speeds of 120 miles per hour, before the parachute is deployed at around 5000 feet. Under the parachute canopy, the jumpers enjoy the stunning views for about five minutes while slowly descending to the ground. This venture was a far cry from Harry's para days in World War II, exiting the plane a mere 650 yards from ground and landing 30 seconds later.

"Hmm," he says, "thinking about it, I would be an idiot to have jumped so long ago on 6 June 1944 and my next jump to be a skydive in front of the cameras of the world on the 75th anniversary of D-Day. So I said to myself, 'You will be smart to have a rehearsal before this', because I'd never done a free fall."

Harry made an appointment with his doctor to discuss his high-flying plans, telling him that he was not only provisionally booked to do a tandem skydive in Normandy on the 75th anniversary of D-Day in 2019 but was also keen to do a rehearsal jump in a few months' time. After giving him a thorough physical examination, the doctor, who was well aware of Harry's medical history and his resolute mindset, gave him the all-clear and signed the necessary paperwork.

Wasting no time, Harry began to make plans for his first parachute jump in 74 years. After making enquiries, it was decided that this would be held at Old Sarum, a former military airfield with a grass runway, two nautical miles north north-east of Salisbury and just 45 minutes' drive from Harry's home in Bournemouth. Utilised in both world wars, Old Sarum was noted for being the best-preserved flying airfield of the World War I period. The airstrip is 11 miles south of Netheravon Airfield, where as a 20-year-old rookie Harry had made his first heart-stopping jump from a glider during his paratrooper training days.

Knowing that two of his granddaughters, Lianne, 37, and Joanna, 39, had previously enjoyed tandem skydiving, when Harry contacted them suggesting they accompany him they jumped at the idea of sharing the thrill of parachuting with their beloved grandad. It was to become a real family affair when, on hearing about their plans, Harry's great-grandson Josh, 23, said he'd also like to be involved. Two weeks before the jump, Josh and his wife Aimee welcomed a baby girl, Isabella, Harry's first great-great-grandchild.

Harry's daughter-in-law Anne, who was at that time The Salvation Army's director of anti-trafficking and modern slavery, realised that Harry's skydiving venture would be a great opportunity to increase awareness and raise funds for confronting this terrible problem head on.

Since July 2011, The Salvation Army has delivered the UK Government's contract to manage support services for victims of modern slavery, with a programme to preserve their dignity, protect and care for them in safe accommodation and provide access to confidential support services.

When Anne and John discussed this with Harry, he was more than pleased to support the anti-trafficking programme, combating what he describes as "a crucial, heartbreaking, worldwide problem". A Just Giving fundraiser was activated in Harry's name for this purpose, with Lianne, Jo and Josh also setting up their own pages. The Salvation Army's Territorial Communications Service also provided support.

"Every aspect of this proposal to jump has been bathed in prayer," Harry wrote on his Just Giving page, "and when my normal common-sense has asked its questions I have the quiet, overruling assurance that our heavenly Father is approving to the degree of being in charge. I don't know how this will glorify him but he is telling me to trust him, and I will."

One of Harry's poems expresses his confidence, referencing Philippians 4:13: "I can do everything through him who gives me strength."

A WELL-PLACED CONFIDENCE

I can do everything through Christ, my Lord:
Those worthy grace-full things that match my dreams;
Those goals employing all his power outpoured,
Effectively fulfilling heavenly schemes.

God has a way of masterminding deeds.
Though works of his are blazed across the skies
He seeks to meet humanity's great needs
By working through our finite hands and eyes.

And I? I can do all he wants of me!
Grace he provides for every step and task;
He gives and gives again abundantly
All that I need – I only have to ask.

In my own strength not much can I achieve,
But Christ reveals himself, when I believe.

When the media first got wind of Harry's planned tandem jump they were quick to realise the newsworthiness of such a good-news human interest story about a 94-year-old World War II veteran committing to a skydive to raise awareness of the scourge of trafficking. Harry was inundated with requests for interviews, both before and after the jump.

On Harry's arrival at the airfield there was high excitement and hugs all around as family and friends, including a minibus-load of his comrades from Winton Bournemouth Corps – plus others who had come by car – cheered him on. Among the crowd were many media representatives with microphones at the ready, eager to interview this man of the moment.

Training took about 30 minutes, including a demonstration of the parachute equipment, instructions about the body position to be adopted when leaving the aircraft and during the free fall, what to expect during the descent, and the best position for the legs on landing. Participants were then issued with a jumpsuit, hat and goggles before being fitted into a harness. Kitted out in their blue jumpsuits, Harry, Lianne, Jo and Josh practised skydiving positions and techniques while in harnesses suspended from the ceiling of the preparation room.

Before he jumped, during an interview in the prep room, Harry explained why he was skydiving: "It has surprised our western world that trafficking is so rife here. That children can be sold, young women – and men – can be trafficked. As the consciousness has risen of this great social need that is actually on our doorstep and worldwide, we ought to be doing something about it. And we are. The Salvation Army's programmes are imaginative and costly, and they're a real ministry to people. There's tenderness, there's graciousness, there's godliness. It's a wonderful project to support."

As Harry walked to the plane for his first-ever high-level skydive, accompanied by his friendly and personable tandem para, Chief Instructor Ryan Mancey of UK Skydiving Adventures, he was cheered on by family and friends, many from the Winton Corps waving yellow, red and blue flags. Lianne, Jo and Josh followed close behind.

The plane took off with a roar and when it was high above the clouds Harry and Ryan made their exit, thrilling to the free fall. As they plummeted through the air at 120 miles per hour before their parachute opened, an airborne photographer came alongside and shook Harry by the hand!

Once the parachute was deployed, during the leisurely descent under the blue and white canopy, with the breathtaking vista below, the photographer again came alongside and Harry took part in a mid-air interview. "What do you think then, Harry?" asked the photographer. "I think it's wonderful … I'm breathless! Absolutely superb!" was the answer. Harry and Ryan's wide smiles during the descent said it all.

"The Press Association had paid for a para-photographer to jump with us," Harry explains. "It meant he jumped slightly before us and was so close we had to take evasive action when we jumped from 10,000 feet, which complicated the start of the free fall. But what skill! Fortunately, I enjoyed every moment of it! The free fall distance of the mile in 30 seconds gives way to the balanced, almost sedate five-minute descent when the parachute opens, with unforgettable views of Salisbury Plain, the New Forest and the South Coast."

Landing safely and exhilarated after the jump, to the resounding cheers of his large crowd of supporters, Harry faced a seemingly endless queue of news agencies wanting to take photos and file their story. In an interview with Channel 4, he commented: "That was superb, and I want you to know that I brought this man down safely," he joked about his tandem partner Ryan, adding that it was a perfect dress rehearsal for a skydive at the next year's D-Day 75th anniversary. He told another interviewer: "It was an easy landing today – the last time I jumped there were some not-very-nice people waiting."

The attendance of the Press Association helped gain widespread coverage of Harry's high-flying escapade. Online, television and radio coverage was also extensive, including BBC News, ITV National News, Sky News, Christian Today, and the Forces Network.

Newspaper articles were effusive in their praise, and the plaudits came thick and fast, with headlines including "D-Day hero, 94, skydives 10,000 ft", "Veteran who parachuted on D-Day takes to the skies again", and "D-Day hero's parachute leap aged 94". *Metro News* wrote: "Meet Harry Read, your new favourite person and life inspiration", *The London Economic* described Harry as "a sprightly, energetic great-great-grandfather" and there were articles in *The Guardian, Christian Today*, Harry's hometown *Bournemouth Daily Echo, Guernsey Press, Scottish Sun, Daily Mail* and *Daily Express*.

Internationally the story was shared in the US by *The Wall Street Journal*, with a photograph of Harry, Jo and Josh featured as their photo of the day, and NBC News, viewed by more than 150,000 people; Channel 7 News and Vision Christian Radio in Australia; media outlets in New Zealand, South Africa, Egypt, Chile and China; and, of course, in Salvation Army publications around the world.

To cap off such a memorable day, Harry happily posed for photographs at the airfield surrounded by four generations of his proud family, including newborn great-great-granddaughter Isabella.

A few days after the jump one of the most warm-hearted and inspirational interviews recorded at Harry's home was with Miracle Street founder Steve Lee, part of a series titled 'Big Story – Amazing Lives'. Miracle Street, a charity, was founded by Steve Lee to "communicate the gospel in a better way to many more people … to inspire and develop churches and travel the country".

The interview began with vision of Harry's recent tandem jump before Steve Lee asked him about his D-Day experiences so many years ago. After recounting the unforgettable events of that epic day, Harry concluded by giving a stirring testimony about his walk with God, including his decision as a 20-year-old paratrooper returned from the frontline in Normandy to become a committed Christian again after losing "the sharp edge" of his faith during military service. "I carried a pocket Bible into battle," he said. "I couldn't see myself not having some connection with God in that situation, although I was not a man of God at that time."

He told Steve Lee that on returning to England his "movement back into the heart of Christianity" was influenced by the example of his elder brother Wilf, and after asking God for forgiveness he realised that he had the assurance of salvation. "I've had a marvellous life – challenging and rewarding – and, looking back over the years, God has always been with me," Harry said at the conclusion of the interview.

The fundraising venture on Harry's Just Giving page was a success. "Money-wise we raised just over £8000," Harry says. "I was so glad that The Salvation Army received a considerable boost around the world. Every report I have seen has been fulsome and generous with our aim to help the cause of trafficked people highlighted."

For some time after the jump Harry was tired but absolutely elated. Sleep didn't come easily for a few nights as he looked forward with pleasure – all being well – to another high-flying challenge just 10 months later.

21

JUMPING TO CONCLUSIONS

"I believe we should not withdraw from a challenge – yesterday is not our best, our best is tomorrow."

~ HARRY READ

Soon after celebrating his 95th birthday, Harry's spirits were high as he anticipated another high-level tandem parachute jump during the much-publicised 75th anniversary celebrations of D-Day in Normandy. When Anne suggested they use the D-Day skydive to again raise awareness and funds for The Salvation Army's anti-human trafficking programs, Harry realised he was jumping for more than just himself.

"The more I thought about human trafficking the more I became aware of the fact that this is truly international," Harry says. "There is not a town, city or country that is immune; it is a worldwide issue. I heard God saying, 'This is not a jump for pleasure; this is a jump to make the world aware of the fact that we need to do something about human trafficking.'"

In April of 2019 Captain Thomas Moore, the famous 99-year-old 'Captain Tom' – later knighted by Queen Elizabeth II – a former British Army officer in the Royal Armoured Corps, was making worldwide headlines by raising money for a group of charities supporting the British National Health Service. His aim was to walk one hundred lengths of his garden in the 24 days before his 100th birthday. A few weeks later the name of Harry Read was also attracting huge media interest with his planned Red Devils tandem skydive over Normandy 75 years after his epic jump as a 20-year-old on D-Day in 1944.

Though earlier in the year battling a digestive problem which caused severe weight loss, and undergoing extensive tests in hospital in February and March, against the odds Harry received the go-ahead from his general practitioner to forge ahead with his D-Day plans. As late as a month before the big day Harry suffered a chest infection and was again required to attend the hospital for more tests.

At the same time, a bevy of big-name media organisations, including the BBC, ITV, Press Association, ITN, Channel 4 and British Forces Television and Radio Service, eagerly sought interviews with this intrepid man. Also requesting an interview were organisers of the Royal British Legion, who had chartered the cruise ship *Boudicca* for a Voyage of Remembrance, with up to 250 veterans, plus their carers and companions, retracing the sea journey made by the armed forces on D-Day, and looking forward to the Red Devils parachute display as the climax of the trip. Harry's tandem jump certainly fired the imagination, with media organisations requesting interviews with him before, during and after the D-Day celebrations.

Before his epic jump, Harry was visited at home by British public-service television network Channel 4 news presenter Jon Snow, accompanied by a cameraman. Proudly wearing his Salvation Army uniform, when Harry was asked if he was nervous about the jump he said with a twinkle in his eye, "I am not in the slightest bit nervous about jumping out of a plane at the age of 95."

"It could be tricky," Jon Snow said. "I prayed about it and I really expected the good Lord to say it's a foolish idea," was the answer. On a more serious note, overcome with emotion at the thought of visiting the graves of his friends and those who had sacrificed their lives in service of their country, with tears welling in his eyes Harry said, "When we go to the cemetery I will not be able to speak but I will weep."

Another of Harry's pre-para jump interviews was with Fred Dinenage MBE, of ITV News Meridien, a veteran broadcaster, journalist and author. "Fred Dinenage turned out to be an excellent interviewer," Harry says. "He had done his homework well and kept a thoughtful touch on the conversation." Fred was to later remark that Harry Read was one of the most inspiring men he'd ever met – high praise indeed from a man who has had a career in television for more than 50 years.

The interview took about 30 minutes and the two ITV cameramen spent another hour or so photographing some of Harry's wartime memorabilia to accompany the filmed conversation. "For some reason they were intrigued by my pay-book," Harry says. "Normally, for security reasons, this was never taken into action because it reveals so much about the soldier's unit but the Allies were so certain of victory they were happy for the enemy to know the units they were facing. We carried them in the breast-pocket of our tunics and mine showed the marks made during the 16 hours I was in the flooded area when landing on D-Day. Even after all these years the 'tide-marks' are clearly visible."

On 1 June, a few days prior to the jump, Harry was a special guest of the Red Devils. It was originally planned just to meet them but their publicity unit requested – and received – a filmed interview. The 75th D-Day celebrations would be Harry's 19th parachute jump since volunteering as a paratrooper at the age of 18 although, besides his first tandem skydive at Old Sarum a few months previously, his last jump was 74 years ago.

As Harry's home in Bournemouth is 172 miles from the airfield in Duxford where the plane flying them to Normandy was scheduled to take off, the Red Devils arranged for him to be transported by car to stay overnight in a hotel at Stevenage, the closest available accommodation to the airfield.

The morning of the 5th dawned and Harry was up bright and early, despite not going to bed until after midnight. It was to be a long day. Anne arrived to pick him up from the hotel and take him on the half-hour drive to the preserved World War II airfield at the Imperial War Museum in Duxford, Cambridgeshire, where they arrived in good time.

The plan was to take off in a Dakota from there at 1.40 pm for a two-hour flight across the English Channel, landing in Normandy at 4.30 pm (French time being one hour ahead of English time). Harry was to take part in a massive display that also included around 280 parachutists re-enacting the D-Day airdrops near Sannerville, with thousands of spectators lining local roads and watching in surrounding fields.

On Harry's arrival at Duxford, there were last-minute reminders and instructions from the Red Devils team prior to their flight and Normandy tandem jump. However, the best-laid plans can sometimes go awry and the Duxford departures were badly delayed because of last-minute issues over technical problems with the civilian plane that was to transport them.

There was concern that the jump might be cancelled, but two replacement aircraft – a Beech 99 and a Cessna Caravan – were hastily arranged by the Ministry of Defence at the eleventh hour. Flight plans for the substitute aircraft were submitted two hours before being approved by the French authorities and the aircraft took off, albeit three hours later than planned.

In the meantime, Harry was introduced to a fellow honorary member of the Red Devils, 94-year-old Scot John 'Jock' Hutton from Kent, who as a 19-year-old was dropped with the 13th (Lancashire) Parachute Battalion near Pegasus Bridge on D-Day. Jock was repeating the tandem jump he first performed five years previously for the 70th anniversary of D-Day in Normandy. Dressed in red jumpsuits and kitted out with full body harnesses, goggles and gloves, Harry and Jock were all smiles as they looked forward to the upcoming skydive.

After being on tenterhooks for three hours, the contingent clambered into the Cessna, with Harry sitting in seat 12, replicating the seat number allocated to him on D-Day. After take-off there was a sense of rising excitement as the Red Devils joked and bantered above the drone of the aircraft. When the plane flew above the English Channel a wave of nostalgia swept over Harry as he recalled the events of D-Day, history's greatest air and sea invasion, so many years ago.

When the aircraft neared its destination at 7.15 pm on a summer evening as mist was beginning to fall, Harry and his tandem partner, Corporal Mike French of the Red Devils team, prepared for their skydive through the clouds. Securely connected at four attachment points – two at the shoulders and two at the hips – Mike and Harry exited the plane to begin their breathtaking descent.

The jump was held over Sannerville, east of Caen, landing in fields at the historic DZ 'K' (Drop Zone K) used as a drop zone for the 8th (Midlands) Parachute Battalion, who went on to destroy bridges in a bid to restrict German movements during the missions on D-Day. As they jumped, thrilling to the velocity of the initial descent, and enjoying the panoramic views of their more sedate drop once the parachute had been activated, vivid memories of Harry's solo parachute jump 75 years ago came flooding back. Against the background of a cloudy sky, he gave the thumbs-up to an accompanying photographer.

The large crowd below, including John, Margaret and Norman, craned their necks to watch the Red Devils' descent, with red smoke trailing their parachutes and one para flying an enormous Union Jack adding to the spectacle. Landing safely in the convoy, including Jock Hutton, Harry was pumped and exhilarated as they were greeted by roaring cheers from spectators lining the field. He was helped to his feet by the Red Devils team, and photographed having a joke with Sergeant Stacey Briggs and being hugged by Margaret before being surrounded by the cameras and microphones of the large media contingent.

Harry could hardly contain his enthusiasm. "I thought the jump was brilliant, absolutely brilliant," he said, "wonderful in every way. I really have to express it in the warmest words. It was a delight. My health is good and my mind is still ticking away. That was superb."

Harry told the Press Association that as he made the jump he was thinking of his brothers in arms who never made it home. "There are very real and definite pleasures in parachuting, but also in my heart I was thinking of my mates. I get very moved when I think about them. I have lived one of the most fulfilled lives that it's possible for a person to live and they haven't."

The morning after the jump, on 6 June, accompanied by John, Margaret and Norman, Harry visited Le Mesnil for a 3rd Parachute Brigade Headquarters D-Day commemoration ceremony, once again marvelling at the peace and tranquillity of the surrounding fields which 75 years ago had seen such death and destruction.

A short service was held in front of officials and military personnel, followed by a wreath-laying beside the former Field Ambulance building. "The highlight of the afternoon," according to military historian Neil Barber, "was the presence of Harry Read, a signaller who actually served there. The previous day he had completed a tandem parachute jump onto DZ 'K'! Harry spent time talking to some of the very interested serving airborne soldiers."

In the evening Harry and fellow D-Day veteran Paul Golz, 94, who had been a conscripted member of the German army, met in the Café de la Digue in Cabourg to mark the anniversary of the D-Day landings. Harry confessed beforehand in an interview with Channel 4 that he was not sure what he would say to Paul, adding, "I do know this, I will accept him. Whatever words I need they will come."

In an introduction to their filmed meeting, the Channel 4 commentator said: "This is the tale of two soldiers who have never met and who were supposed to kill each other 75 years ago on this beach – one fighting for the Führer and the Fatherland, Paul Golz, aged 18 on D-Day; the other fighting for King and country, Harry Read, barely a year older."

The day before their meeting, while Harry was making headlines with his Red Devils tandem skydive, Paul Golz visited the German war cemetery at La Cambe in Normandy, replete with thousands of black stone crosses. Afterwards he was interviewed on a beach close to where he and his fellow soldiers surrendered to an American tank crew.

Paul remembered the shouts of US soldiers at that time: "Hey boys, come on, let's go; this war's over for you!" Paul and his fellow POWs were marched to Utah Beach and loaded onto a British ship. He became a prisoner-of-war in Scotland and the US and after his release learned English before joining the diplomatic service.

In a memorable encounter, when Harry and Paul were introduced, Harry said to him, "I'm so glad to see you and to shake your hand, and say bless you. We are partners. Once we were on a different side, but now we are partners together – in the rebuilding of the world." "Of course," Paul replied. "We understand each other."

Afterwards came a poignant and evocative moment when the two veterans shook hands again as they farewelled. "Now we are friends," Paul said to Harry. Placing a hand on his shoulder, Harry replied, "We are more than friends, we are brothers."

The next morning Harry and John joined the Airborne tour group and made the ferry and coach trip back to Portsmouth after two taxing but unforgettable days. On arriving home, during the next few days Harry was inundated with more interviews, letters, cards, emails, Facebook messages and phone calls congratulating him on his recent parachuting exploit. He also personally received many donations to the anti-trafficking programme which he passed on to the Just Giving organisation. In his two tandem jumps Harry raised a total of £20,899, donated by 850 supporters.

While his story had spread far and wide, there was also huge interest in Harry's hometown of Bournemouth, with numerous phone calls from people asking Harry to speak to their school, club or organisation about his time in Normandy. As well as neighbours expressing their admiration, Harry's postman congratulated him on the jump and told him he had pinned photos of the event on the noticeboard in the Post Office refreshment room. When Harry went to do his shopping, the taxi driver recognised him and they had a chat together.

It could be concluded that Harry's skydive at the 75th anniversary of D-Day was the crowning glory of his nonagenarian years but just a few weeks later there was another accolade in store for him.

Though he didn't go out very often at night, Margaret persuaded Harry to attend the commissioning celebrations of the Messengers of Compassion session held at Westminster Central Hall on Saturday 6 July. Because he had spent so many years in leadership at the Training College and had mentored thousands of cadets during that time, Harry was pleased to attend.

The commissioning meetings were led by the UK territorial commander, Commissioner Anthony Cotterill, and during the evening General Brian Peddle took to the platform. "I'm here under false pretences," he announced to the crowd, "because I want to show you something. It's a very beautiful video that we want to show today to pay tribute to an incredible gentleman, Commissioner Harry Read." The camera pivoted to where Harry was sitting with John, Margaret and their families, and caught him completely taken by surprise.

The video recalled Harry's service as a paratrooper in World War II, followed by his lifetime of service as a Salvation Army officer. It also included his Légion d'honneur award, and his recent D-Day skydive in Normandy followed by his meeting with Paul Golz, with Harry's comment to Paul, "We are more than friends, we are brothers" warming hearts once again. Why was the video being shown on this occasion? Commissioner Harry Read was about to be awarded the Order of the Founder.

To sustained and affectionate applause, Margaret helped Harry negotiate the stairs to the platform where he and General Peddle exchanged reciprocal Salvation Army salutes, and Harry acknowledged the acclaim of the crowd.

The Order of the Founder is the highest and most prestigious award the international Salvation Army can bestow upon a Salvationist. The honour was instigated in 1917, five years after the death of William Booth, to recognise exceptional service by Salvationists, whether officers or soldiers. In more than a century, less than 260 have been awarded.

Harry's service ticked all the boxes regarding the criteria, not least his Christ-like spirit, eminent service as a Salvation Army officer, and making such an impact on social media. Specifically, the criteria are:

- Outstanding service above and beyond the call of duty: This was exemplified throughout Harry's more than 70 years of officership, including writing *Words of Life* for 10 years in retirement.

- Pioneering or innovative work of an exceptional nature: Inspirational Training College leadership for a total of 18 years, including writing songs and pageants.
- Personal sacrifice in the interests of the Army: Many and varied examples throughout his officership, including spending much time in his Facebook ministry to almost 5000 friends
- An identifiable, unique contribution to the ministry of the Army: Distinguished service as a Salvation Army officer in corps, Divisional Headquarters and Training College appointments, and international leadership on three continents.

The Order of the Founder award consists of a certificate bearing a brief account of the order, a concise record of the recipient's service, and bearing the General's signature. A medal in the shape of a shield bearing a likeness of the Founder, William Booth, with the inscription 'Service memorable' is also awarded.

In presenting Harry with the award, the General said to him, "In recent years you've been a bit of a problem for me. This is the first time I can recall that an Order of the Founder has been influenced by social media [cheers from the audience], and in fact that the pending recipient would have such an impact through social media." The General added that he also had a social media presence and, he said to Harry, "All of your fans have been making suggestions to me, as if I can't make good decisions on my own," prompting peals of laughter.

As he handed the framed citation of the Order of the Founder to Harry, General Peddle remarked on his incredible influence through many years of faithful service. The citation read: "In recognition of a life of outstanding Christian witness in word, verse and deed spanning 75 years, with a recent and relevant witness through social media captivating a global audience with the authentic message of reconciliation, hope and peace."

After the General took some time pinning the Order of the Founder medal to Harry's uniform, eventually saying, "I think I got it!", Harry quipped: "You got my third rib," which again brought more roars of laughter from the crowd.

On receiving the award, Harry responded from the heart. "I count it a very great privilege and honour to be made a member of the Order of the Founder … I've enjoyed life so much. I've lived a full life and I'm grateful for all the love and support that has come my way over recent years. I feel almost guilty about that jump, you know," he added, referring to his D-Day tandem parachute jump a few weeks earlier. "If the way of sacrifice is the way of sacrifice I feel guilty because I enjoyed every minute of it!"

As the crowd erupted in a standing ovation, the joyful conviviality and outpouring of love and admiration for Commissioner Harry Read OF seemed almost palpable, and his award was met with widespread acclaim. Amazing grace! Amazing faith! Amazing fortitude!

A live stream of the meeting ensured that thousands of people from around the globe shared in the occasion. Many responded with words of congratulation on social media, with comments including: "Just having breakfast in Melbourne and saw this on Facebook. It has made my day." "Commissioner Read … is a spiritual giant who has achieved so much in a long life, and continues to serve faithfully. I can't think of anyone more deserving." "An enduring inspiration, Christian leader, gentleman and all-round top bloke." Afterwards, a social media wit suggested that it would have been appropriate for Harry to make his entrance to Westminster Central Hall on a zip line!

At the conclusion of the meeting Harry was inundated with well-wishers and then met up to celebrate with members of his family before John drove him home to Bournemouth, two and a half hours away by road. After about four hours' sleep he was up and about early the next morning in order to attend the Sunday morning meeting at Winton Corps, where he was again greeted with hugs and handshakes. "I hope the corps officer didn't notice, but I fell asleep in the meeting," Harry says.

22

ONWARD AND UPWARD

That man is a success who has lived well, laughed often and loved much.

~ ROBERT LOUIS STEVENSON

The year 2020 was nominated by *Time Magazine* as "one of the worst years to be alive" in modern history, with the burgeoning COVID-19 pandemic causing mayhem across the globe. In this dystopian disaster, bereavement, face masks and lockdowns became the new normal but, not surprisingly, 96-year-old Harry Read faced the challenge with characteristic wisdom and faith.

"The coronavirus is serious and must not be underestimated but even in this situation God is multiplying his grace beyond all measure," he says. "Past experience comes to our aid, memories are enriched, comfort is received, and by God's grace we can give comfort to others. He has more than enough grace for all circumstances."

In these troubling times, still living independently, Harry was assisted not only by his family but also his many friends from the Winton Bournemouth Corps, who developed a practical programme of keeping in touch with comrades, especially the elderly. "My phone was also very busy and I had much to occupy my mind and heart," Harry says.

Following lockdown rules, Harry was not allowed any visitors but resolved to take time for a walk each day to Horseshoe Common, in the vicinity of his flat. While treading carefully, his trusty walking stick made reassuring sounds." I tried to greet everyone I met," he says, "and most people were warmly responsive but so many these days are engaged in conversation with the palm of either one of their hands."

In the meantime, Harry's digestive problem had worsened significantly but he faced the extreme and distressing challenges with typical resourcefulness and fortitude, declaring that, "The 'essential me' is fine and the Lord's hands are holding me." His increasingly arthritic fingers also presented problems but that did not deter him from persevering at the computer keyboard with his Facebook ministry and correspondence with his many friends.

Still in demand by the media, Harry was one of a number of D-Day veterans interviewed by British newsreader Sonali Shah as part of the Royal British Legion contribution to the 75th anniversary of VE (Victory in Europe) Day. Because of the coronavirus lockdown at the time, Harry was interviewed by phone, recounting his D-Day experiences while the livestream broadcast included photographs supplied by him.

Just four weeks later, on 6 June, Harry was featured in an online service of remembrance to commemorate the 76th Anniversary of D-Day and the service of the 6th Airborne Division and Allied forces in Normandy. Filmed beforehand because of coronavirus restrictions, Harry read the stirring words of 'For the Fallen' by Laurence Binyon:

They went with songs to the battle, they were young,
Straight of limb, true of eye, steady and aglow,
They were staunch to the end against odds uncounted;
They fell with their faces to the foe.

They shall grow not old, as we that are left grow old;
Age shall not weary them, nor the years condemn,
At the going down of the sun and in the morning
We will remember them.

This left Harry reflecting on the power of words. "'Age shall not weary them, nor the years condemn' – it is almost as though the writer was looking for something positive to say about an early death in battle," he says. "Age hasn't wearied me, nor do I feel my age condemns me. Those who died in battle haven't been spared the rigours of life; they've been deprived of life's opportunities and joys. That surely is the tragedy of our military cemeteries."

Later in the service, to the sombre but beautiful strains of 'Nimrod', from Sir Edward Elgar's 'Enigma Variations', the camera followed Harry as, smartly dressed and wearing his red beret and medals, he walked to place a wreath in the gardens outside his home before giving a salute to the fallen.

On 26 June, Harry's long-time friend Lieut-Colonel Norman Bearcroft passed away aged 94 at his home in New Jersey in the US, and Harry was invited by Norman's son, Major Mark Bearcroft, to contribute to the online festival of thanksgiving for Norman's life.

In his heartfelt tribute, Harry commented on Norman's warm personality, his creative friendship, his many timely words of encouragement and his brilliant, seemingly never-ending, flow of inspiration. "As long as we live," Harry said, "we who are privileged to be friends of Norman, will cherish our friendship and cannot but feel that, when we meet again in our heavenly home Norman will just happen to have a new manuscript and a suitable instrument for us to play for our heavenly Father's honour and glory."

Still seemingly indefatigable at 96 years of age, Harry's book, *Language of the Soul: The Mystery and Power of Prayer*, was self-published in 2020, with the cover design by John and the e-publishing expertise of granddaughter Lucy, who lives in New Zealand. *Language of the Soul* is available both as a hard-copy book or an ebook.

The introduction speaks for itself: "This book accepts the mysteries of prayer, its comfort and power to change attitudes, lives and circumstances. Quite amazingly, God wants us to pray, not only because it has a calming confidence-building effect on us, but because he sees us as partners in his world-redeeming strategy for bringing an alienated world back to himself."

Prayer has always been a priority for Harry. "I treat prayer as the dominant feature of my life," he says. "As soon as I wake up I am making a prayer, and when I go to bed I am making a prayer, winding up the day. I have my set times for prayer during the day and my prayer lists are very lengthy. When I have a poem that I've been sorting out for Facebook, I say, 'Can I rest in you, Lord, in the light of what this poem is saying?'"

Many of Harry's prayer poems are written in sonnet form, made up of 14 lines of 10 syllables, with the last two lines encapsulating the message. It doesn't take a large stretch of imagination to sense that Harry's God-given poetic prowess is reminiscent of the masters:

William Shakespeare: "Let me not to the marriage of true minds admit impediments…"

Elizabeth Barrett Browning: "How do I love thee? Let me count the ways…"

Harry Read: "Lord, I thank you that your love is mine; More fresh than dew, more pure than mountain stream..."

EVERLASTINGLY LOVED

Lord, I thank you that your love is mine;
More fresh than dew, more pure than mountain stream,
A love that all your qualities combine,
A love surpassing any human dream.

Your love is tender, patient and so strong,
It knows the worst yet falters not at all;
Sees through my weakness, challenges the wrong
And seeks each baleful influence to forestall.

I am the object of your loving care!
All that is best for me your love has planned;
No circumstance need drive me to despair
Since I am held securely in your hand.

I am much loved – loved everlastingly,
And love you, Lord, for having so loved me.

Each poem in the book has a prologue and an epilogue, with a biblical reference. In this case the prologue reads: "The fruit of the Spirit is joy! (Galatians 5:22) and the epilogue, "Just thanking God for Jesus who said to his disciples, 'I have told you this is so that my joy may be in you and that your joy may be complete'" (John 15:11).

Musing on his writing discipline over the years, Harry says, "Writers tend to be aware of the fact that perhaps they could have done better. We can spend oceans of time revising and revising and the average reader would have been well-satisfied with our first or, at most, earlier revision. Our search for the right word or sentence sometimes makes us subject to the despotic mind-set of perfection."

THE WIT AND WISDOM OF HARRY READ

Harry's pithy comments about his insights as a nonagenarian are indicative of his faith, positivity and unquenchable love of life under God's hand. His testimony speaks for itself and the following quotes from this man of God cannot fail to inspire and bless.

"It could be concluded that my life is dull and uneventful but such is not the case. In my prayers each morning, and then again in the afternoon, I travel the world as I move through my prayer lists. By prayer I'm permitted the privilege of sharing in the ministries and struggles of officers and others as they face the many challenges that are theirs. How our good Lord achieves this I'm not clever enough to understand or articulate properly, but it seems to me that, as the Holy Spirit strengthens, equips and uses them, our prayers add qualities of faith, vision and achievement."

"Prayer is a spiritual partnership that our heavenly Father considers vital or he wouldn't have planned it that way. What a privilege! What joy and fulfilment! I don't need to open my door and leave my flat to be an encourager on a world scale."

"It is no sacrifice for me to 'keep on keeping on' as far as work is concerned, as I have an anti-lethargy prayer strategy. By and large, I only do the things I like doing but my problem is that I like doing so much which perhaps gives the impression that I'm a driven man. My major regret is that I'm slowing down and my memory is not as accurate as it once was. Names, for instance, were my speciality but not anymore. Somewhere on my desk is a little note reminding me that I'm Harry Read."

"My 'shuffle off this mortal coil' fills me with no apprehension! I've had a wonderful life and the life to come must be so much better. Our heavenly Father, whose imaginative approach to creation fills us with wonder, must have something incredibly spectacular waiting for us in the life to come. In the meanwhile, I must continue to use my time as wisely as possible before I experience that 'in the twinkling of an eye' moment. Imagine! One moment trying to remember my computer password for this, that or the other, and the next moment, with all the brightness of mind and athleticism of spirit, bounding towards the pearly gates."

"Obviously, aches and pains come and go but I can think of no good reason for my extended lifetime. Maybe the good Lord isn't ready for me yet! Facetiously, I tell my friends that the City Council has just renewed my bus pass and I wouldn't want to waste that."

"I have had, and am still having, quite a marvellous life, with each day bringing its fulfilment. As the years go by, a positive attitude helps hold back the effects of the calendar."

"How important we oldies are as role models. We enable the younger generations to see that the all-sufficient grace of our Lord is exactly that. They can look at us and be encouraged by the fact that at whatever stage we are in life we can live it triumphantly."

"The writing gift might qualify as a hobby, because I've written quite copiously over the years: articles, scripts, songs and poems.

I follow cricket and football on television but make few sacrifices in my following."

"I've had a whale of a life … God has given me so much. A wonderful wife, a beautiful family, countless friends, a marvellous job – all a man could ever wish for."

"Over the hill is not such a bad thing; after all, going downhill is a lot more fun."

"When in 1949 I was stationed alone as a young Salvation Army lieutenant, I had the special insight that I was responsible for my own morale. It is a maxim that has helped shape me through the years, never more so than in the years since Win went to heaven. My morale, therefore, even in difficult times, is usually high."

"My slowing down is gathering pace. I spend half my life pressing wrong keys on the computer and the other half apologising for my incompetence. The third half is creatively employed and the fourth half has me smiling smugly with pleasure. I'm not very good at maths either."

Harry celebrated his 97th birthday on 17 May 2021, receiving more than a thousand warm and loving greetings on Facebook. Looking back over the years of his remarkable life, Harry says: "I'm now the oldest person ever in my clan. I suppose longevity is in the genes." Thinking of his brothers Wilf and John, and sister Lucy, Harry speaks with understandable pride.

As previously mentioned, his older brother Wilf joined the British Army in 1938 and became a commissioned officer, serving mainly in the Middle East, for some time on General Bernard Montgomery's staff. On demobilisation in 1945 he joined the staff of one of Britain's largest firms, eventually becoming company secretary. "Of we three Read boys I think he was the most remarkable; his gift range was immense," Harry says.

Harry's sister Lucy married a Baptist minister, Reginald Spooner. Their son, Harry's nephew, Dr David Spooner, is one of the top cancer consultants in the country. "David is a delightful Baptist," Harry comments, "and when made a consultant was the youngest ever in the UK." In 2021 David received an exceptional contribution award from the Royal College of Radiologists.

Harry's younger brother John was able to go on to further education and became a top accountant, a partner at the age of 30 in the London office of Price Waterhouse, before moving into the wider commercial world. His brief included the chairmanship of two prestigious consultative groups for UK Prime Minister Margaret Thatcher.

When Harry was invited to be an entrant in *Who's Who*, he discovered that his brother John and he shared the same page. Harry's entry read: "Born 17 May 1924; s of Robert and Florence Read; m 1950, Winifred Humphries (d 2007); British Commissioner, Salvation Army 1987–90; Editor, Words of Life, 1992-2002."

"I have no idea why *Who's Who* asked me to join their honoured club," Harry says. "I certainly didn't seek the distinction. When I was British Commissioner we had a pretty high-powered advisory board and maybe one of the members set the ball rolling. I'm glad it happened because a number of very good things have followed because of that exposure that have been good for the Army and its witness."

While pleased that his brother John shared the distinction, Harry was disappointed that his older brother Wilf was not also included, convinced that because of his stellar life and influence he deserved the same accolade.

"Forgive my pride in my family," Harry says, "but our upbringing in our little depressed northern industrial town hasn't done us very much harm. I'm almost haunted by the fact that my forebears must have had latent gifts desperate for nurturing and expression, but which had to be surrendered to the insistent needs of feeding and bringing up the family," he muses.

"Many a Tennyson, Isaac Watts and the like must have walked behind a juddering plough and the back-ends of a couple of horses. Their task was to concentrate on straight lines, instead of allowing their imaginations and spirits to roam and harbour the fruits of freedom of thought and create a legacy of devotion and inspiration. Our debt to the past is immense."

And it's not only his siblings and forebears that Harry is proud of. Win was the light of his life – highly intelligent, grammar school educated, teachers college graduate and deputy headmistress before being called to become a Salvation Army officer. "Win was one of the most remarkable women you could imagine," Harry says. "She had a very creative mind and could converse with anyone at any time."

Son John, Major (Dr) John Read, was The Salvation Army's ecumenical officer for the UK and chair of the territory's moral and social issues council before retirement. He and Anne served as corps officers in large industrial cities in the north of England and southern seaside locations. They also undertook educational appointments at London's William Booth College and New Zealand's Booth College of Mission, John as principal and Anne as senior training officer. John is the author of *Catherine Booth: Laying the Foundations of a Radical Movement*, published by The Lutterworth Press.

Harry's favourite (and only) daughter Margaret has a qualification in pastoral supervision and served as a corps officer with husband Graham at Crawley, Barnsley, Dunfermline, Pokesdown, Southhampton Scholing and Cannock until his promotion to Glory. Following her marriage to Norman, they were appointed as divisional leaders in the London North East Division, which became Herts and Essex Division after a reorganisation in 2016. Margaret and Norman entered well-earned retirement in 2021.

The next three generations of the family – four grandchildren, Mike, Joanna, Lianne and Lucy (and their marriage partners,

Tanya, Steve, Paul and Tim); 11 great-grandchildren, Josh, Nyah, Niamh, Ethan, Elise, Cole, Hudson, Jude, Rosa, Ramona and Juno; and three great-great-grandchildren, Isabella, Amelia and Georgia, are a beautiful legacy of Harry and Win's abiding love.

As for their Salvation Army 'family', thousands of people would readily testify to the lifelong influence Harry and Win had on their lives. With service spanning four decades, including Training College, corps, divisional, international and British leadership appointments, followed by such an active retirement, their contribution to the mission of The Salvation Army is immeasurable.

In the years following Win's passing, Harry's caring personality, incurably optimistic nature, unbridled courage and vibrant faith, coupled with his prayer and Facebook ministry, have endeared him to Salvationists around the world.

Reflecting on his blessed and joyful life in more than 70 years as a Salvation Army officer, Harry says, "The challenging, adventurous times I spent as a soldier in the paras have been more than matched by the very different – but still very challenging and adventurous – life of faith I've lived as a soldier of Jesus Christ. To be part of his mission for a needy world is a highly privileged vocation.

"Looking back on a long life of service I can say gladly and truthfully, 'My cup has never been less than full and running over.'"

EPILOGUE

Commissioner Harry Read has left an indelible mark on the lives of those of us privileged to have known him, loved him, worked with him and shared life with him.

~ GENERAL BRIAN PEDDLE

As the final touches to *Wings of Faith* were being made, Commissioner Harry Read was promoted to Glory on 14 December 2021 at the age of 97 years, following a fall at his home a few weeks earlier.

Messages poured in from around the world, reflecting the deep love and affection of those who recalled Harry's inspirational influence on their life through his wartime bravery as a young man; his service in The Salvation Army with Win as a corps officer, Training College leader and mentor, and leadership in Canada, Australia and Britain; 10 years of writing *Words of Life*; his thousands of Facebook poems; and his parachuting exploits at the age of 95.

A Service of Committal was held at 11.30 am on 17 January 2022 at Bournemouth Crematorium. In moving moments Harry's coffin was carried by a bearer party from 216 (Para) Signals Squadron while a bugler played the Last Post. Corporal Mike French, Harry's partner in their D-Day 75th Anniversary skydive into Normandy, was also present to honour his memory.

Then followed a Service of Celebration at Winton Bournemouth Corps at 1 pm, led by Commissioners Anthony and Gill Cotterill, leaders of The Salvation Army in the United Kingdom Territory with the Republic of Ireland, who also led the Service of Committal. The sounds of the Reveille echoed through the citadel at the beginning of the service, which was shared online, watched by thousands who joined in celebrating Harry's life and legacy.

'The Finale: A Service of Celebration', was prepared by Harry himself with the same meticulous care and preparation he took in all aspects of his life. Ever the wordsmith, he wrote a number of songs and poems especially for occasion.

Loving tributes were given by Harry's family, John and Anne, Margaret and Norman – who each read one of Harry's poems – and two of his grandchildren, Jo and Mike, who wrote his own poem about his Pops. Their words revealed the love and devotion they shared with Harry.

John: "Dad was astute, bold, creative, determined, enthusiastic, faithful, generous, humble, innovative, just, kind, and oh so loving." "Dad enjoyed a splendid life – marvellous, glorious – and yet his horizon embraced the life beyond, yet more splendid, even more glorious."

Margaret: "Dad was always supporting and encouraging." "He was my hero … he remains my rock … he was often my confidant … and such a prayer warrior."

Jo: "Granddad was a man devoted to the service of others … generous, kind, loving and present." "Every opportunity for kindness was relished. He understood that time was a gift and he gave that gift joyfully."

Mike (excerpts from his poem 'The Evolution of a Man'): "Harry trained and he flew, he jumped from the blue – and he grew into a warrior" ... "Harry and Win loved and they laughed and they danced on their path – and they grew into parents" ... "They nurtured and cared and they loved and they shared – and they grew into leaders."

Isabella, 3 (recounted by Margaret): "Pops, you're incredible!"

One of Harry's songs close to his heart was sung to the tune of Blaewern:

Love has conquered – evil vanquished,
Love in triumph reigns supreme.
We, who once in darkness languished
Have the lights of freedom seen.
Love, God's nature, came revealing,
Bringing gain where once as loss,
Making mercy all-appealing
Through the anguish of the Cross.

Love has conquered – O so tender
Is its touch on every heart,
Granting heavenly peace and splendour,
Bidding sin and stress depart.
This is love that shares each burden,
Lifts the scales from anxious eyes,
Speaks the healing words of pardon,
Tells of Christ, the heart's true prize.

Love has conquered – death defeated
In the tomb where Christ was laid.
Calvary's aims have been completed;
We can face death undismayed.
Not for him, or us, sin's prison,
God has rolled the stone away.
Love has conquered! Christ is risen!
Evermore is Easter Day.

Harry's nephew, Major Alan Read, read messages from Commissioner Keith Banks: "Harry was one of my dearest friends, whose courageous and visionary spiritual leadership helped me to grow in grace"; Colonel Derek Elvin: "Harry's adventurous and creative mindset remained with him whatever his position"; and General John Larsson, who declared that Harry was his model, his mentor and his friend. "Harry was multi-gifted … a great encourager."

Another poem written by Harry, and read by Norman during the service, reveals his indomitable faith, no matter the circumstances:

This ageing process moves relentlessly,
It seems as though, a day past yesterday
Was when I sought and found true liberty,
My few emerging gifts allowed full sway.

But now, with movements slow and wearisome –
Aware that energy has evanesced
I march to life's slow, intermittent drum
And, by the simplest things, I'm hard-pressed.

But age is not dependent on the mind.
The Spirit helps to keep us ever young,
The spirit's power in us is unconfined
And tunes our hearts to Heaven's timeless song.

I cannot older be than timeless grace
Then, up and on, I must run Heaven's race.

Winton Band played an excerpt from the selection 'Songs of the Soldier', featuring 'God's Soldier', and the Songster Brigade sang 'Become Aware of Him' – two iconic songs from Harry's inspired pen. Leah Shave, a young member of Winton Corps and a prayer partner and friend of Harry's, read selected verses from Romans chapter 8.

A tribute from General Brian Peddle, who was overseas and unable to be present, was read by Commissioner Cotterill. The General commented: "Harry was spiritual giant ... He had depth of spirituality, a genuine relationship with God and a depth of understanding that benefited all who have read or sung his words ... He was one of a kind."

Commissioner Cotterill was the final speaker at the Celebration Service, which had earlier included a video of Harry's life from childhood to his nonagenarian years. "Our appreciation of all things Commissioner Harry Read, Order of the Founder, Chevalier Légion d'honneur, is immense. We salute his faithfulness, his courage, and daring to be different."

The service ended with the triumphant singing of 'God's Soldier', the atmosphere encapsulating Harry's life of vitality and faith. With a mix of joyfulness and poignancy the words rang out: "We're going to fill the world with glory ... We're going to turn the world upside down."

A traditional Airborne Forces benediction was then read: "May the defence of the most high be above and beneath, around and within us, in our going out and in our coming in, in our rising up and in our going down, through all our days and all our nights, until the dawn, when the sun of righteousness shall rise with healing in his wings, for the peoples of the world, through Jesus Christ, our Lord. Amen."

Wings of Faith honours Commissioner Harry Read – his courageous and caring heart, unwavering faith, poetic gifts and irrepressible love of life, as well as the enduring example he bequeathed to countless numbers of people because of his exemplary life and Christian witness during more than 70 years of service as a Salvation Army officer.

Harry's coffin carried by a bearer party from 216 (Para) Signals Squadron

Harry's Service of Committal at Bournemouth Crematorium

The more we see of death, the more we know
That death is a beginning, not an end;
The final barrier through which we go
Our destiny to find and comprehend.

Life has no meaning if love dies with death,
If, like our flesh, its qualities can waste;
Our hearts remind us: love breathes Heaven's breath
Since God with timelessness our love has graced.

For death is but the soul returning home;
The well-worn key that opens up the door
Where love beyond imagining is known:
For Heaven is home – now and for evermore.

INDEX

C

D

E

F

G

H

I

J

K

L

M

N

O

P

Q

R

S

T

U

V

W

Y

BIBLIOGRAPHY

Davies, Howard. *Words and Music: Stories Behind the Songs.* Melbourne. Salvo Publishing, 2017

Gariepy, Henry. *General of God's Army: The Authorized Biography of General Eva Burrows.* USA: Victor Books, 1993

Gariepy, Henry. *Mobilised for God: The History of The Salvation Army Volume Eight 1977-1994.* USA: The Salvation Army, 2000

Larsson, John. *Saying Yes to Life: An Autobiography. London:* Salvation Books, 2007

Merritt, John G. (ed.). *Historical Dictionary of The Salvation Army.* USA: The Scarecrow Press, Inc. 2006

Noland, Joe; Court, Stephen. *Tsunami of the Spirit: Come Roll Over Me,* USA: Crest Books, 2014

Read Edward. *In the Hands of Another: Memoirs of Edward Read.* Canada: The Salvation Army Canada and Bermuda, 2002

Read, Harry. *Heart Talk: The Give and Take of Communion with God.* Melbourne: Salvo Publishing, 2013

Read, Harry. *Language of the Soul: The Mystery and Power of Prayer.* Self-published, 2020.

Read, Harry. *No Heart More Tender: A Book for the Bereaved from a Christian Perspective.* London: Salvation Books, 2010

Read, Harry. *Words of Life: The Bible Day by Day (1992-2002).* Hodder & Stoughton (now an imprint of Hachette), for The Salvation Army IHQ

SALVATION ARMY PUBLICATIONS

Journal of Aggressive Christianity. Court, Stephen

Salvationist, The Salvation Army UK and Ireland

The Musician, The Salvation Army UK and Ireland

The Song Book of The Salvation Army, London: Salvationist Publishing and Supplies

The War Cry, Australia

The War Cry, USA

The Salvation Army Year Books, Salvation Books IHQ

Printed in Poland
by Amazon Fulfillment
Poland Sp. z o.o., Wrocław
30 October 2022

5444699d-2f46-46ff-bf68-9fc97a23f81fR01